OLD WRONGS
NEW RIGHTS

STUDENT VIEWS OF THE
NEW SOUTH AFRICA

OLD WRONGS
NEW RIGHTS

STUDENT VIEWS OF THE
NEW SOUTH AFRICA

Edited by Dan Connell

Africa World Press, Inc.

P.O. Box 1892
Trenton, NJ 08607

P.O. Box 48
Asmara, ERITREA

Africa World Press, Inc.

P.O. Box 1892
Trenton, NJ 08607

P.O. Box 48
Asmara, ERITREA

Book design: Melanie Klaus-Martin, Nikki Panagiotaris,
    Kady Shea, and Sheila Sheedy/Studio 5, Simmons College
Front cover art & cover design: Kady Shea

Library of Congress Cataloging-in-Publication Data

Old wrongs, new rights: student views of the new South Africa /
edited by Dan Connell.
    p. cm.
  Includes bibliographical references and index.
  ISBN 1-59221-628-5 (hard cover) -- ISBN 1-59221-629-3 (pbk.)
  1. South Africa--Politics and government--1994- 2. South Africa--Race
relations. 3. South Africa--Social conditions--1994- 4. Blacks--Civil
rights--South Africa. 5. Minorities--Civil rights--South Africa. 6.
Human rights--South Africa. 7. Apartheid--South Africa--History. 8.
Women college students--United States--Biography--Anecdotes. 9.
Women college students--Travel--South Africa--Anecdotes. 10. South
Africa--Description and travel--Anecdotes. I. Connell, Dan.

    DT1971.O43 2008
    968.06--dc22

                                                    2008005456

To the activists
who work today to build
a New South Africa

To support organizations and projects described
in this book, send your tax-deductible check earmarked for
Simmons projects to:

South Africa Development Fund
555 Amory Street
Boston, MA 02130

Contents

Introduction 9
   By Dan Connell

Personal & Political Rights
Gays and lesbians navigate a complex society 17
   By Victoria Latto
Lesbians: Equal if you can afford it 22
   By Paula Bettencourt
South Africa's first 'feminine,' not 'feminist,' legal association ..26
   By Elena Larson
South Africa a base for refugees seeking democracy elsewhere 29
   By Christina Lenis

Economic Rights
Apartheid legacy lingers 37
   By Erica Fields
Waiting for water 40
   By Christina Lenis
Waiting for housing 44
   By Beth Maclin
Shack-dwellers contend with more than cold 50
   By Lucìa Cordón
New houses are not enough 54
   By Paula Bettencourt

Social Rights: Education
Get-rich-quick mentality dominates urban youth 69
   By Lucìa Cordón
Helping street kids: Small NGOs do it better 74
   By Erika Fields

Who they are is the question—not where 78
    By Faythe Mallinger
For street girls, success is relative 82
    By Kristin Pitts

Social Rights: Health Care

Fighting the twin demons of HIV and rape 87
    By Victoria Latto
Drugs, rape and HIV—South Africa's perfect storm 92
    By Elena Larson
TAC takes on HIV/AIDS 95
    By Erika Fields
South Africans push government on HIV/AIDS 99
    By Beth Maclin

Cultural Rights

Art as personal struggle 119
    By Kristin Pitts
Art as politics 123
    By Faythe Mallinger
Art as activism 126
    By Ashley Price

Reflections

At home in their home 131
    By Faythe Mallinger
Riding the teeter-totter 134
    By Kristin Pitts
A walk in a different light 138
    By Christina Lenis
Never forget 144
    By Ashley Price

Appendices

Simmons College 151
The Itinerary: May–June 2007 156
Contacts in South Africa 160
Notes on the Contributors 163
Acknowledgments 165
About the Editor 166

Introduction

Apartheid, the intricate system of racial domination that defined South Africa for a half-century, was designed not only to codify a hierarchy of privilege among the country's diverse population groups but to create wealth for those who ruled, to micromanage the social and cultural lives of their subjects, and to squelch any sign of dissent before it could turn into revolt.

It was a form of tyrannical rule more akin to the divide-and-rule strategies of nineteenth century European imperial powers than to any form of modern-day discrimination. The main difference was that in this instance the colonizers were in-country rather than overseas-hence its characterization by anti-apartheid activists as "internal colonialism." Looking at it from this perspective helps us to understand the baggage the newly democratic nation carries today.

Apartheid's draconian body of laws reached into the most intimate aspects of peoples' lives-what jobs they could hold, where they could live, whom they could sleep with. Like any despotic system, it became ever more sinister as it came under challenge from those under its heel-and from people of conscience within its own ranks. But resistance built up steadily and won support around the world. By the mid-1980s, with its prisons swollen with political opponents, apartheid began its retreat.

Some of the system's most egregious laws were rolled back ahead of the unbanning of the underground African National Congress and the release of Nelson Mandela from prison in 1990. More laws fell before 1994 when, after protracted negotiations, the white minority finally ceded power to the ANC in the country's first multiracial elections. What few remnants remained were swept away with the ratification of a new Constitution in 1996 that guaranteed all South Africans equality under the law.

But apartheid was more than a means of segregating people

and excluding the majority from the political process. It was also a mechanism for whites to harness blacks to work in their mines, their farms, and their industries and to tend their gardens, clean their houses, care for their children and much more, all at bare subsistence wages-in short, to serve them in all spheres of their lives while reaping none of the benefits of their labor. Could the mere repeal of bad laws, the promulgation of new rights, and the transfer of political power remedy these manifest wrongs?

Clearly not, and few, if any, South Africans would suggest that they did.

Yet South Africa today is almost as deeply divided as it was in the 1980s, with the majority still mired in extreme poverty while a minority, albeit it a more multicultural one, maintains a standard of living that compares with that of Europe or North America. Unemployment runs over 50 percent among black youth, many of whom lack the education, training, or skills to pull out of it. Half the population lives in shacks, most of which lack electricity and running water, let along a safe source of heat.

A visitor is immediately struck by these contrasts, not only between those living in white and black neighborhoods, but also, as several of the articles here reveal, within the black and "colored" townships. South Africa embraces both the first and third worlds within its own borders-and in its very identity. As one student observes, this induces an almost schizophrenic response-which is the real South Africa, she wonders? Can both be true and still this be one nation?

It is no longer the law that sustains these grotesque differences; rather, it is the inertia of circumstance. It is the legacy of apartheid. It is what it is because it was before-and will not be otherwise unless people make it so. What we learned is that old wrongs only give way to new rights after a fight—and a sustained one at that.

But, the students asked, what-or who-holds back change today? Who is trying to propel the society ahead, and why does so much remain to be done? What difference does it make to have a visionary constitution that not only guarantees every citizen full participation in the political process, but also rights to housing, health care, education, personal security, and a safe environment if people do not actually enjoy these rights now?

This book records what they learned about South Africa-and about themselves—in the process of seeking answers.

The Trip

We arrived in Johannesburg, the country's largest city, at 7:30 a.m. on Monday, May, 21-eleven women from Simmons College in Boston, Massachusetts, with diverse academic and social backgrounds (see Notes on the Contributors), and me, their bedraggled professor. After nearly twenty-four hours of travel, we were exhausted but yet eager to jump right in. Few napped once we arrived at our Mayfair guest house.

Over the next week, we visited museums and historical sites dedicated to preserving the apartheid experience-and the broad-based, multiracial resistance to it—for future generations; we toured African townships, workplaces, and homes; we met with government officials, party cadre, academics, activists, and ordinary South Africans; we interviewed representatives of cutting edge social movements and nongovernmental organizations (NGOs) and observed their practice; we took time out for excursions to a game park north of Jo-burg and to the nature reserve at Cape Point; and we talked frequently among ourselves to process our experiences along the way.

We also heard about the rights struggles of other Africans—notably Eritreans and Zimbabweans—who now make their home in South Africa due to fear of persecution in the lands of their birth, much as South Africans did through the decades-long fight against apartheid. That these exiled activists come here to find sanctuary while continuing their fight for rights at home was one sign of what South Africa's democratization means for the continent. That the ANC government has been reluctant to support their causes says much about what happens to revolutionary ideals once those who hold them ascend to power.

Nevertheless, we found that South Africans have gone through profound changes since the apartheid era, in both the substance of their lives and in the ways they think about themselves, their nation and their future. Whatever disappointments people have faced, whatever backsliding there has been, South Africa is not today what it once was. But it is not what many activists imagined it would be by now.

Enormous gaps remain between the promise and the reality.

Many South Africans have stayed hopeful, but a growing number are becoming impatient with the sluggish pace of change, and a core of activists have taken up the methods of protest honed during the anti-apartheid struggle to push a more aggressive social change agenda.

One of the most dynamic that we observed was the Treatment Action Campaign (TAC), founded in 1998 to both protest the government's anemic response to the HIV/AIDS epidemic and to mobilize people at the grassroots to do something about it from below. Among the other new movements we met were the Soweto Electricity Crisis Committee and the Western Cape Anti-Eviction Committee, which work on housing, electricity, running water, sewage, public safety, and other community issues.

But we also saw signs of a younger generation growing up with no experience of the anti-apartheid struggle or the democratic culture and vision that arose from it. Many are not only impatient but not political and do not expect anything more but what they see in front of them, which is not good. One avenue through which this alienation plays out is street crime, now at record levels. Another is drugs, whose use is skyrocketing. Thus, we found, the clock is ticking.

The Book

Old Wrongs, New Rights is divided into sections that correspond to the themes of our research, rather than a chronology of the trip. We start with enquiries into personal and political rights and move through economic and social rights to culture and the arts. The last section is memoir-style segments where writers were given free rein to reflect on their experience and share with the reader how they were affected by it.

Victoria Latto and Paula Bettencourt open Section One by tackling the issue of gay and lesbian rights, not just as they are spelled out in the Constitution-one of the few in the world to ban discrimination based on sexual preference-but as they are actually experienced. They find the issue inextricably entwined with race and gender, as lesbians of color face far different threats to their safety and dignity than do white lesbians or gay men of any racial background.

Elena Larson sits in on a revealing discussion among women lawyers who seek to use the newly egalitarian atmosphere to push for greater gender equality in their profession, still a bastion of male prerogative where highly skilled women receive half the pay of male counterparts. They do so with wry humor and self-deprecation as they interview public relations pros on how best to project themselves to the public.

Christina Lenis, who filmed us throughout the trip, explores the experience of Eritrean exiles who use the Web and satellite radio to mobilize their compatriots to support human rights and democracy in their homeland, even as they face a rising tide of anti-immigrant feeling in South Africa.

In Section Two, Erika Fields, Christina Lenis, Beth Maclin and Lucía Cordón take a hard look at the ways apartheid's legacy lives on in the critical field of housing in the burgeoning black townships and shantytowns around South Africa's cities. We meet Aunty Gertie who, faced with eviction, decided she had had enough and stood up to the authorities, from which she learned that when politeness fails, protest still works. We stroll through a Soweto squatter camp where the stark contrasts between rich and poor confront a visitor on a street by street basis, and we learn of the dangers many shack-dwellers face from a man whose shack went up in flames from an open fire they built to keep warm, taking his sister's life and nearly killing him. But new houses may not be enough, says Bettencourt, who finds that new money, not repressive laws, now drives people out of family homes and destroys traditional communities.

In Sections Three and Four, we look at social rights, concentrating on education and health care, which receive strong support in the Constitution. Cordón talks with a former gangster about his campaign to reach at-risk young black men in the townships before they lose themselves to a life of drugs and crime, as he almost did. Fields, Pitts, and Faythe Mallinger give us complementary takes on the pioneering work of Ons Plek, a shelter for street girls, and Latto, Larson, Fields, and Maclin examine the HIV/AIDS epidemic and the contrasting approaches coming from innovative social movements like TAC and the remarkably obtuse ANC government.

In Section Five, Pitts, Mallinger and Ashley Price give us three perspectives on the obstacles black South Africans have faced in pursuing their passion for art, from politics during the apartheid era to economics and culture today. All three pieces draw on

13

encounters with women artists at the Funda Community College in Soweto, where director Charles Nkosi observed that art is "the blessing of being able to share your experiences with other people."

Mallinger, Pitts, Lenis, and Price wrap up with reflections on the trip-and how it changed them. Mallinger will never again look at a low-income neighborhood and see only what is not there. Pitts and Lenis confront their initial discomfort in Khayelitsha and find themselves moved by the strength of family and community despite the humble surroundings. And Price finds searing echoes of her family's experience as African Americans in the Cape Town Slave Lodge where apartheid South Africa and the Jim Crow South are joined in back-to-back exhibits.

We leave South Africa-and end this book-convinced that he struggle for human rights for others is at its most essential a struggle for our humanity as well.

Dan Connell
Boston, Massachusetts
December 2007

Personal & Political Rights

Gays and lesbians navigate a complex society

By Victoria Latto
Pilanesburg, South Africa

Vervet monkeys chase each other up and down trees. The screams of guinea fowl and "go-away birds" reverberate in the distance. But nature competes with nurture for the attention of passers-by.

A blonde woman in a pink layered top, her arm snaked around the back of a taller woman with spiky bleached hair, sunglasses, and a black T-shirt, searches her car for a pack of cigarettes.

"I still think it freaks out a lot of people," says the woman in pink, who gives her name only as Sintel.

But, she adds, "I suppose they're getting better."

What people are getting better about, says Sintel, is seeing two women in a relationship. She and her partner are visiting Pilanesberg Game Park for the weekend, and they have been sitting on the grass in each other's arms, speaking to each other in Afrikaans, as other park visitors sneak peaks at them while viewing the wildlife.

This year, South Africa became the fifth country to legalize same-sex marriage, under orders to do so by the Constitutional Court. But while the country's new constitution, ratified in 1996, is the most progressive in the world when it comes to gay and lesbian issues, public perception is not always reflective of that.

Sintel says her mother "freaked" when she came out as a lesbian. She says coming out was difficult because of her "staunch Afrikaans" background, but that her family is now more accepting of her sexual orientation.

Still, says Sintel, "we don't talk about it."

Sintel wears a silver cross around her neck—her "good-luck charm"—and attends a gay church in Boksburg, a suburb of Johannesburg, South Africa's largest city. Such churches, she says, are rare.

Religion has been a force to be reckoned with in both the old and the new South Africa. Most South Africans are Christians, though there is a sizeable Muslim minority in the Cape Town area and a Hindu minority in the Indian Ocean port of Durban.

Much as Christianity was used to both validate and condemn apartheid during the dark era of the National Party rule from 1948 to 1994, it is now used by both pro- and anti-gay Christians to make their cases.

Marlow Valentine is a living example of this.

"My journey with gay rights started when I struggled with my own sexuality," says Valentine, now a Community Outreach Coordinator.

Valentine grew up in Heideveldt, a township designated by the apartheid government for "colored" people (those of mixed race). His family, he says, was Christian and very conservative.

Torn between his faith and his emerging knowledge that he was gay, Valentine discovered the Metropolitan Community Church (MCC).

The MCC is a worldwide organization with nondenominational churches on six continents. Its congregations, which have a focus on social justice and human rights, are open to everyone—regardless of sexual orientation.

Through his activist work with MCC, Valentine says he was recruited by the Triangle Project, a Western Cape nongovernmental organization focusing on gay, lesbian, bisexual and transgender (GLBT) issues.

"Our main focus is to empower people," says Valentine, adding that the Triangle Project focuses on healthcare, well-being, safety, counseling, and public education. Since its policy is to not duplicate what other GLBT organizations are doing, it does much of its work through partnerships with other advocacy organizations across the country.

One such partner is the Equality Project, with which Valentine has also been involved. He says that during South Africa's tumultuous transition to democracy, the Equality Project lobbied for sexual orientation to be included in the new constitution.

In 1996, they succeeded: Sexual orientation was included in the non-discrimination clause of the Bill of Rights.

And in 2006, the Civil Union Act—mandated by the Constitutional Court after a lengthy campaign by advocacy groups—gave same-sex couples the right to marry, as well as access to the same legal protections as heterosexual couples.

"The gay and lesbian movement has achieved more victory than any other marginalized group," says Jody Kollapen, head of South Africa's Human Rights Commission.

Today, says Kollapen, the challenges that the GLBT movement faces are more social than legal.

The Civil Union Act has been "a vehicle to speak about prejudice" in a larger context, says Valentine.

But, he adds, "the amount of prejudice that exists in society as a whole is also reflected in the gay community."

Valentine points to large discrepancies in GLBT acceptance along racial and economic lines.

The posh Waterkant neighborhood of Cape Town serves as the gay Mecca of South Africa, with bars, clubs, and cafes that cater to a mostly white, gay male clientele.

Lesbian nightlife in Cape Town is not as easy to find. But at the club nights that do cater to women, the audience is heavily white. "More and more women [of color] are accessing these spaces, but not enough," says Valentine.

Valentine says there is a GLBT community in the townships as well—particularly a drag queen and crossdresser subculture in "colored" townships and a butch lesbian presence in black townships. "Unfortunately, those social spaces in townships are very limited," he says.

Many people in the townships—established far from the whites-only downtown areas of most cities during the apartheid era, often through forced removals of entire black and colored neighborhoods—lack the resources to come into Cape Town for socializing and support systems. Even for those who do have transportation to travel the twenty-plus miles into the city, they risk being marginalized by a mostly-white gay mainstream.

However, for GLBT people of color, the townships carry their own risks.

In 2006, nineteen-year-old Zoliswa Nkonyona was gang-raped and killed in Khayelitsha, a township outside Cape Town. Nkonyona was an out lesbian.

"We are targeted because we are lesbians. Men see that as an invitation to rape," Thso Gcakafi tells the *Mail & Guardian*, a newspaper in Johannesburg. Gcakafi was a friend of Nkonyona's.

"Lesbians in South Africa face abuse and violence simply for not fitting social expectations of how women should look and act," says Jessica Stern, a researcher for Human Rights Watch's LGBT rights program. While this can hold true for all races, it is even more pronounced for lesbians of color.

One pervasive myth in the black community is that homosexuality is "un-African" or a Western import, say local activists.

"It's one of the stereotypes we're very vocal about," says Valentine. Homosexuality, he adds, is "as African as Africa is."

Valentine says there have been same-sex relationships throughout South Africa's history, especially among the men who worked together in the mines and were forced to live in same-sex hostels and among the women who were left behind in the rural areas when their husbands migrated to find work.

Valentine says the Triangle Project tries to create safe spaces in townships, instead of taking people out of their comfort zones.

Another area in Triangle's field of vision is schools. Over the next three-to-five years, Triangle is launching a new initiative focused on youth. Its education programs are not only for students, but for teachers as well—making them aware of issues their GLBT students may be facing.

Valentine says the Triangle Project wants to establish "a culture at schools of having an inclusive approach—not something where they [GLBT youth] are labeled or further marginalized but where they can be affirmed as human beings."

Part of the youth initiative includes HIV prevention among teenagers. "HIV/AIDS is still pandemic in the gay community," Gordon Isaacs writes in the Triangle Project's newsletter.

The gay community is not alone: South Africa as a whole has one of the highest rates of HIV infection in the world. However, most of the studies done on HIV in the country are focused on pregnant women at risk of passing the virus to their children. Few studies have been done on HIV among gay, lesbian, bisexual, and transgendered people.

Valentine says that in light of social problems like HIV/AIDS, poverty, unemployment, and violence, GLBT issues can pale in comparison. "Basic needs are not being met in rural areas, let alone gay rights," he says. But this does not mean such issues ought to be ignored or treated separately, as they, too, are part of a larger project to democratize the country at all levels.

Today, says Isaacs, "there is a sense of looking at human rights issues around gay men and women rather than the political structure that was fought for in the past."

Valentine, too, emphasizes a shared commitment to human rights for all. "I simply refuse to be defined as a man who only has sex with men," he says. "It's my humanity that defines who I am."

Lesbians: Equal
if you can afford it

By Paula Bettencourt
Cape Town, South Africa

Estrogen dominates in this arena.

Curves, hips, breasts writhe and flow to the beat of the music. Space gets squeezed and bodies begin to touch as the dancing intensifies. The crowd locks together to the whip of the DJ, free of inhibitions.

On the dance floor, women monopolize the crowd. At the bar, women line up to get their drinks. In the booths, women sit and laugh gaily, the loud music pumping in the background. There is not a man in sight.

Shorthaired bois, goth queens, cosmetic femmes, and those in-between flock to the Junction Café for Lush, an occasional club-within-a-club that convenes here by and for women who love women.

"This is the only place for us," Ame Manim says over the din, her voice broadcasting anger and frustration. What makes her mad is that the café only hosts the gathering every other week, leaving women like her with very little nightlife, especially where they can meet other women. She says there are no alternatives.

Being gay and a woman in Cape Town is severely limiting, even though this city is known as "the gay capital of Africa." For most lesbians in urban South Africa, however, the experience is one of invisibility, even within the greater gay, lesbian, bisexual, and transgender (GLBT) community.

Under the racist system of apartheid that defined this country for decades, gays and lesbians were discriminated against regardless of their skin color. Being a homosexual was illegal. During the struggle to end racial oppression, gays and lesbians fought for their right to live freely as well.

With the ratification of their post-apartheid constitution in 1996, South Africa became the first country in the world to guarantee equality of sexual orientation. The constitution also guarantees gender equality, promising a gay woman equality with a gay man under the law. But paper rights do not automatically translate into equality in daily life.

Gays and lesbians say they are still discriminated against in the country, and within the gay community women say they are also disadvantaged.

Lush is the last women-only nightclub in the city, with the other gay bars and clubs all male-oriented or male-dominated. This leaves little room for women to carve out their own place. And apart from the nightlife scene, there are no other women-only venues in the city.

In the greater LGBT community, many gay-oriented places advertise themselves as "mixed," yet they are frequented mostly by men and are focused on what men want, says Manim.

On gay-oriented Web sites such as the Triangle Project, an LGBT community service organization (www.triangle.org.za), and on social-networking sites like Mamba Girl (mambagirl.com) and gay South Africa (www.gaysouthafrica.org.za), the majority of postings, articles, and advertisements are for gay men.

Myrna Andrews, the originator and manager of Lush, says women are "nesters"—they get into a relationship and stop going out, which is why there is very little out there for women. However, in a series of personal interviews, many women at Lush expressed the desire for more venues and more women-oriented groups.

Olwen Nel, Andrews's girlfriend and partner in organizing Lush, says gay men and women do not get along. "The gayer the girl goes, the less she takes care of herself; the gayer a guy goes, the more care he takes," she says.

This appears to put the divide squarely on superficial characteristics. But others disagree.

Manim describes the scene as dominated by men, especially at mixed events such as the annual Cape Town Pride Week in February. She says women are discouraged from participating equally because men hold the power in these areas and activities are focused on their needs. A similar event lasting a week every October in Johannesburg, South Africa's largest city, is chaired by a prominent lesbian, though most events are male-oriented.

Perlisa Mantuse agrees that gay women are more invisible to visitors than gay men. "They would see a gay [male] community if they came to Cape Town, definitely," says Mantuse, a lesbian who works at Lola's, a popular Cape Town vegetarian restaurant owned and operated by a gay male couple.

Staff members of the Triangle Project, an outreach organization that works for equality through education rather than advocacy, say they see this discrepancy between men and women as well. Marlow Valentine, the community outreach coordinator at the project, says there is discrimination against women in the greater community, but that there is also discrimination against subgroups within each sex grouping.

He says there are two "groupings" for women— one a venue for women of color called Hectic and another, Pussys on Fire, which is a mostly white social group that goes clubbing in mixed nightspots in the city. But, according to Andrews, Hectic moved to Stellenbosch recently, leaving Lush as the only club for women of any color in Cape Town today.

Valentine also says there are striking differences among lesbians regarding their openness about their sexuality within the black and "colored" townships and between these townships and the city. In black townships women are more open about being gay, he says, and they frequent local shebeens [bars], while in the "colored" townships women are more closeted.

But as black lesbians move more freely in the townships, they take on more risks, Valentine says. This leads to higher rates of rape and murder in these areas, often motivated by anti-gay sentiments—what would be termed "hate crimes" in the United States—according to the Triangle Project, which is attempting to curb such attacks by educating people to accept diversity in sexual preference, especially in partnership with schools.

Valentine says there is a divide not just between the gay men and women, but also between whites and non-whites among gay women. Part of the reason for the racial divide is economic and part social, he adds, citing difficulties finding safe and affordable transport for women of color to the gay nightspots, nearly all of which are in predominantly white areas.

This is seen at Lush, where, on a June evening, more than 90 percent of its patrons are white. According to one black woman who asked to remain anonymous, she would never go to Lush if she still lived in a black township because it is too expensive and dangerous to travel out of it at night.

She also says the atmosphere at Lush is welcoming to her, despite the fact that she is one of the few black women present, and she does not feel uncomfortable there, even though she knows others who would.

"It is harder to be a black lesbian in a mixed crowd, where being a women makes me stand out too," she says.

Andrews says she tries to get a more racially mixed crowd and has a small loyal following who are black. She says that race is no longer an issue for those who go out clubbing, but that it is the reality of their daily lives and the separations built into them that keep racial divisions alive.

Under apartheid Cape Town was segregated along strict ethnic lines designated by the government. Blacks and "coloreds" were moved out of the city center to townships set up along racial lines. These townships are still in existence today, and their demographics are little changed. Khayleitsha and Langa residents are still mostly black, while those who live in the Cape Flats remain almost all "colored."

Most people living in these townships cannot afford to move into the city, says Valentine. Socially, there are few places for lesbians in the townships to get together in public, and when they do, they risk their lives, he says.

The new constitution guarantees equal access to housing, along with political equality under the law, but economic redress in a society yet characterized by a greater gap between rich and poor than almost any other country in the world is a slow process—one that holds back many lesbians from moving out of the townships.

Those few who are able to afford it can mix with whites in the lesbian-friendly urban arenas, if they can get there—and if they can find a venue once they do. "The problem is that there is nowhere for us to go," says Manim.

South Africa's first 'Feminine,' not 'Feminist,' Legal Association

By Elena Larson
Cape Town, South Africa

"Men can't join officially," Seehaan Samaai says with a smile, her silver bracelets jingling as she points to the only man at the table of women. "So he's our associate member."

The table erupts with laughter as Samaai removes her yellow scarf and adjusts her wrap dress with a smile. The other women at the table take off their cashmere pashminas and coats and pour cups of tea with nods of agreement.

As they take their seats, the meeting of the Western Cape's chapter of the South African Women's Legal Association (SAWLA), South Africa's first and only legal association for women, comes to order.

The association was founded in May 2006 to unite, empower, and increase the number of women in the legal professions, as women and people of color are still largely underrepresented in the field, says Samaai.

Though it has been eighty-four years since white women were barred from the legal professions here, forty years since women of color were formally kept out, and thirteen years since the fall of apartheid—best known for its draconian structure of racial domination but also characterized by rigid patriarchal values—gender representation remains unequal in the legal profession, as it does in many others.

While South Africa's constitution carries clearer and more sweeping guarantees of gender rights than any other constitution in the world, the country still struggles to implement affirmative action and other initiatives to realize the goal of full equality in practice.

For its part, SAWLA's organizational constitution commits the group to advance women lawyers in the new egalitarian atmosphere of post-apartheid South Africa, recognizing that the country's starkly unjust past continues to negatively impact women's access to justice and equal protection under the law.

This evening's SAWLA agenda includes choosing a public relations agency to plan the Western Cape chapter's upcoming launch party. In accordance with their basic principles, they have agreed to appoint a women- or black-owned company to plan the launch.

As one woman reviews the profile sheet of the ones contending for the contract, she stops short at a black-owned agency that boasts a commitment to social equality. "They claim to be such a progressive company, and they have one woman—only one," she says with raised eyebrows. "We'll have to ask them about that."

Samaai, a prominent lawyer, professor of law at Western Cape University, and founding member of SAWLA, says that women in the legal professions face many barriers. They include entering the profession and finding work, achieving a sufficient income equal to that of a male in the same position, and sustaining employment.

There are two women for every one man in law school in South Africa, yet there are significantly fewer female lawyers than male, according to Samaai, and even fewer women judges and heads of superior courts. "Women do not have a voice in policy dialogues," she says. "They need to empower themselves."

And empower women, SAWLA does. Its key programs include leadership and professional development trainings for women, especially in the fields of research and writing. A group of women activists launched a History and Icons Project alongside SAWLA to identify and honor the women who have engaged with the law to make a difference in the lives of women and others.

Participation in the women's movement is encouraged, too, though Samaai says that feminism is a touchy subject. "Feminism isolates people," she says. "We are all mothers, sisters, professionals—we don't need to be hardcore."

Samaai, herself, is a wife, mother, and professional. At the age of thirty she has been married for more than twelve years and developed her own law career alongside her husband's in filmmaking. "We built our good years together," she says with a serious expression. "My family always comes first."

Samaai describes the order of her typical day and says that time with her two children every morning is among her most important priorities. "Time with my children is non-negotiable," she says, using a term borrowed from her professional life to describe her family life. "Everyone knows this. My mornings are for my children and my afternoons are at the office."

Samaai says that most of the other SAWLA members feel similarly. "We worry about our cases and also about daycare," she says, adding that "feminism" is unpopular because it suggests independence from men and family, which is not true of many of the women lawyers associated with SAWLA.

"We want to address all women," Samaai says.

Two young women of color who own one of the public relations agencies say they believe just that, when it is their turn to present their plans.

"Feminine, not feminist" is their mantra. They suggest reds and pinks as the colors for the launch. They say that beauty products should be in the goody bags. And they propose to update SAWLA's signature graphic—the scales of justice—to include a decorative heart.

"Women multitask," says one. "That should come through in your event."

SAWLA's meeting comes to a close at 7:30 p.m. after the members select the "feminine, not feminist" agency to organize their launch. They say they were disappointed with the black gentleman who represented the so-called "progressive" company—and are ready to head home to their families.

One woman stops at the door and turns to face the group.

"Hey, I think that woman is the baking powder lady on TV, yeah?" she asks about one of the women of the "feminine" agency.

"Right!" they respond. "I thought so!"

"She can cook anything," one says to Samaai.

"That fits with our image," Samaai says with a smile, as the rest of the group breaks into laughter.

South Africa: A base for refugees seeking democracy elsewhere

By Christina Lenis
Cape Town, South Africa

Four neatly dressed African men sit patiently in soft chairs on the seventh floor of a posh downtown hotel overlooking the boutiques and upscale restaurants that dot the Victoria and Albert Waterfront. But none of them is here as a tourist.

They are members of the Eritrean Movement for Democracy and Human Rights (EMDHR), an organization of refugees and exiles from the small northeast African state of Eritrea, formed in 2003, whose mission is to raise public awareness about the extensive human rights violations in their troubled homeland.

In 2000, they came to South Africa as students along with 600 other Eritreans on scholarships from the World Bank. Seven years later, they are still here, now seeking political asylum. They say their country—Africa's newest nation—is slipping deeper and deeper into despotism under a ruthless dictator who has kept Eritrea in a state of constant conflict with its neighbors while brutally cracking down on dissent, all in the name of "national security."

The EMDHR now plays a leading role among Eritrean refugees and exiles around the world by means of print publications, a Web site (www.emdhr.org/), and radio programs in the Tigrinya language that they relay to listeners by satellite. They also run workshops for Eritreans in South Africa, and they attend human rights conferences elsewhere in Africa and in Europe, according to a spokesperson for the group.

But it is the newly secured rights to free speech and unfettered political activity here in South Africa—unique on the continent— that inspire this work even as they make it possible.

Eritrea, a former Italian colony with a 600-mile coastline on the Red Sea, was swallowed up by landlocked Ethiopia in the 1960s. Eritrean nationalists fought a thirty-year war for independence against successive U.S.- and Soviet-backed Ethiopian regimes before winning it in 1991 and installing the former liberation movement commander, Isaias Afwerki, as the country's new president. But Eritrea went back to war with Ethiopia in 1998 over border issues and has remained in active confrontation ever since, with United Nations troops keeping the two sides apart but with the prospect of renewed war never far away.

The year after these men came to South Africa, they say, their government rounded up hundreds of protesting university students and sent them to a desert work camp where several died of the heat. Soon afterward, the government, facing criticism for refusing to implement a constitution ratified in 1997, shut down the independent press and began arresting all its critics, including government ministers and former independence army veterans.

Today, the example of South Africa's long and difficult fight for democracy gives these men hope—as well as a base of operations for waging their own fight to change things at home.

South Africa is the best place to do this, according to Emanuel Tsefayasus, who says he can experience here what he can only dimly imagine anywhere else he has been. He also gets to meet people from all over the world, which is very different from what he experienced at home as his country became more and more isolated and inhospitable to foreign visitors, and he can organize his compatriots with no fear of retribution.

"You experience a bite of the whole world in South Africa," adds Buruk Tekle, who says there are now thousands of Eritrean refugees here and more coming on a daily basis to escape the deteriorating political situation at home.

However, they face new problems once in South Africa where they may wait years for work permits, even as they encounter resentment from some South Africans who accuse them of taking their jobs. Many refugees set up informal businesses in order to survive, selling cheap consumer goods in the streets and hoping to avoid getting robbed or mugged by the army of criminals that operate there.

"As a refugee, you have to put a lot of effort to get a small change in your life as compared to the citizens living here," says Tekle.

Tekle says he is now engaged in a complicated process to become a recognized refugee with defined rights under South African law. As a registered asylum seeker, he says he is granted the right to work and to study. But he quickly adds that in the workforce, xenophobia thrives.

"Discrimination is always on the menu in South Africa," says Yared Tseguy. "They have this race issue that's still living."

Tseguy says that South Africans treat other Africans differently, stereotyping them according to where they are from just as others did this to them under apartheid, when race and ethnicity determined everything from where people lived and worked to whom they could date and what beaches they could use. And, he adds, the bureaucracy is so elaborate that it must have been set up to stop people from getting refugee status.

South Africa's Department of Home Affairs tells him that, as an asylum seeker, he does not need a special work permit, he says, and that the basic working papers they give him will be sufficient when applying for a job. However, when he has tried to do so, he says that employers invariably ask to see a proper work permit.

The Equal Employment Act, designed to help South Africans disadvantaged under apartheid, discriminates against foreigners, he says. Individuals are hired based on the principle of "reparation" for past wrongs, giving blacks, "coloreds" and women an edge, but other Africans fend for whatever jobs are left—if any.

With a constitution that promises basic human rights to all its people, South Africa has become a model of democracy and an inspiration for him and for thousands of other Eritreans, says Tekle. But he wishes these principles would be applied to everyone in South Africa today, regardless of their national origins.

Meanwhile, he hastens to add, the situation is far worse where he came from.

"No new fresh ideas are accepted, and there is no room for negotiation on any issue," says Tekle, who insists that this makes democratic change impossible in Eritrea. "We are not free because we are not guaranteed [any] rights that are taken for granted in other parts of the world."

Tekle compares Eritrea to the darkest days of apartheid. He says his government not only denies people freedoms of speech, press and assembly, making protest impossible; it sharply limits what religion they can practice, and it restricts all movement inside the country, as well as travel in or out of it. It also requires all unmarried women and men up to age forty-five to participate in an open-ended "national service," which can mean military duty but also places thousands of conscripts in unpaid jobs for businesses owned by the government or the ruling party.

In 2005, the U.S. named Eritrea a "country of particular concern" because of its religious freedom violations. Religion, however, is just one aspect of the country controlled by the government. "You have no control of your life," says Tekle. "You grow-up and you have to fit wherever the government tells you."

The EMDHR started by publicizing human rights violations in Eritrea. Members moved on to describe the experiences of refugees—why they were leaving their country and what they faced once they were out. Today, they are a civic movement with the goal of raising awareness of and respect for human rights principles among Eritreans at home and throughout the world.

EMDHR members say they want the atrocities in Eritrea to end, but in a peaceful way. "We don't want to change things with force," says Tekle. "We are a non-violent civic movement."

Through their educational projects, they say that such awareness is steadily growing. And they say they are free to do all this because of the rights they enjoy in South Africa.

Satellite-based radio programming is listened to throughout Eritrea and is the most difficult form of communication for the Eritrean government to control, according to Tekle, who says that EMDHR's twice-a-day broadcasts have a large following.

"Our radio is mainly a civil action," says Tekle, who hopes this will inspire his beleaguered sisters and brothers at home to take action for their rights, much as South Africa has inspired him.

"Let's rise and say, 'No, we don't want this anymore, we have to change the country,'" he says.

The Cape Town chapter of EMDHR is trying to get a book published in their national language, Tigrinya, on the stories of political prisoners in Eritrea. In 2005 they helped other EMDHR chapters create the magazine *Meseley*, which promotes non-violent action against the government in order to get back their rights.

"We want to educate the people. We don't want to paint political ideas on anyone because the paint might go off the next summer. We don't want to do that—we want some permanent solution to the problem," says Tekle.

"If the people understand what's going on, change will come, because it will come from within everyone, from within all Eritreans, and I wish the impact could hit all of Africa because other African brothers and sisters are also experiencing the same problems," says Tekle with a gleam in his eye.

"We wish that everyone in Africa could think about rights. We believe that the will of the people is the most powerful thing—that is what we are trying to achieve," says Tekle. "We have this opportunity, and we want to use this opportunity."

"This is just a start," he adds. "We can make demonstrations because we are living in a democratic country in South Africa, but we hope we will one day carry these demonstrations to [the Eritrean capital] Asmara, and everyone can join us."

Economic
Rights

Apartheid legacy lingers

By Erika Fields
Langa, South Africa

The room is painted light blue with bright blue doors and windows. Blue plastic chairs line the back wall, along with stacks of extra tables and supplies. The setting evokes images of peace—or perhaps sadness. Or maybe just the water for which our host fights.

The woman people call "Auntie Gertie" takes off her shoes and tucks them under her chair, as she settles in. Her black skirt and black-and-white striped shirt balance her black-and-white headscarf. Her gold and silver bracelets shake as she talks.

There is no money to build the houses, according to Gertrude Sharp, who heads a grassroots protest group called the Western Cape Anti-Eviction Campaign. The government has the land, just no money, she says.

The Campaign—one of many new social movements to arise when apartheid ended and the African National Congress came to power—was established in 2000 in this overcrowded black township outside Cape Town to help poor South Africans forced out of their houses when they could not pay their rent. Today, says Sharp, it works to stop evictions and water cut-offs, improve the community's poor health services, fight for free electricity, and end police brutality.

But for all this, Sharp's involvement is still deeply personal.

Sharp says she grew up living in a tumbledown shack in Athlone that offered little protection from the elements. "When it rained, it didn't just leak into the shack," she says, "it rained into it."

She says she had to leave school at age twelve to find work to help support her family. Then in 1990, with three children of her own, she was forced to move from the Athlone squatter camp to new rental housing in Langa. But, earning barely $5 per week for cleaning houses, she could not keep up the payments and feed her children, too.

One day in 1991 she came home from work at 6 p.m. and found all her furniture on the ground outside her small house, now locked up tight. She had been forcibly evicted.

Sharp says she had a key with her, so she moved everything back in and snuck out the next morning at 5 a.m. so officials would not see that she had returned. Then she went to the township council to protest. They gave her a few hours to come up with the money, which she did.

"It was a long time ago, but it feels like yesterday," she says.

A month later, she says, she had trouble coming up with the rent, and she again came home from work to find everything she owned in the street. Once again she borrowed the money to cover what she owed and got back in.

But when her furniture was removed for a third time, she says she had had enough. "I sat outside the door watching my children playing in the street," she says, " and I decided I was going back in, and I would not move out at dawn."

The next day she went to the council and told them she was not prepared to go through this again. She says she gave them her small pay slip and said: "You tell me how to work this out."

When they replied that this was not their business, she says she became furious: "I said I have nowhere to go, and I am not carrying my furniture out of that house again." And off she went, looking for higher authorities in Cape Town to tell her story.

After sympathetic provincial officials ordered the local council to leave her in her house, she says, other township residents began to seek her advice when they had problems. When in 1999 the council evicted an eighty-three-year-old old woman who could not see or walk by herself, neighbors gathered in the street and ran to fetch her.

"As they were carrying the furniture out, we were carrying it back in," she says. "That is how I got involved." After this incident, they formed the Anti-Eviction Committee.

Today, says Square, the housing situation for many poor South Africans has worsened even though the race-based restrictions on where people could live that were imposed under the apartheid system are now gone.

The Groups Areas Act of 1950 required people to live in specified areas according to their racial classification: white, "colored" (people of mixed race), Asian, or African. Under another law, whites, who comprised less than 15 percent of the population, were allocated more than 80 percent of the land.

Anyone from outside the correct category was to be removed. In the Cape Town area alone, 18,000 people classified as "colored" were forcibly relocated between 1964 and 1969, according to government estimates. One racially diverse community near the center of the city—District 6—was dismantled altogether. A museum that seeks to keep this history alive sits there today.

"The Groups Areas Act instituted the division of urban areas into separate townships, which were designed to divide and isolate communities," says a District 6 Museum brochure. "Poorly constructed working-class townships were built, separated by buffer strips consisting of freeways, polluted rivers and *vleis*, and strategically placed military land and golf courses. In District 6, apartheid's grand design was to remove 35,000 people from the city's core to its distant periphery."

The end of apartheid in the early 1990s brought the curtain down on formal racial separation, but it did little to resolve the enormous economic disparities that today keep most black South Africans in shacks, despite promises of decent housing for all in the 1996 Constitution.

Housing problems have worsened for many due to increased transport costs and scarce employment, while the wait for new government-supplied housing is extremely long. Meanwhile, families grow larger, more poor people migrate into the cities, and existing houses become more crowded. "And there was no progress in making the houses bigger for families that have grown over the past twenty years," says Square.

So, she says, families are starting to take matters into their own hands.

"Communities are calling for the government to put promises to work," says Square. "We want to know what happened to the democracy."

Waiting for water

By Christina Lenis
Langa, South Africa

Whiteboards covered with English and Xhosa greetings stretch across a classroom wall. Newspapers sit under a window waiting to be recycled. A tiny brown tick moves slowly across the floor.

A middle-aged black woman sits in a chair, holding a book in her hand, staring into space. "The government will do something when it suits them," she says at last.

Gertrude Square, or Auntie Gertie, as she prefers to be called, is talking about water—clean running water and toilets for her community in the bustling black township of Langa, twelve miles from Cape Town, the country's legislative capital and a popular international tourist destination. And about how she mobilized her community to demand what they were promised.

For a growing number of impoverished black South Africans, gaining political equality in 1994 was not enough. They also want the government to fulfill the pledge of social, economic and cultural rights guaranteed by the 1996 Constitution.

As the leader of a new community group, the Western Cape Anti-Eviction Campaign, born during a series of demonstrations over the eviction of township residents unable to pay their rents while waiting for houses promised by the new government, Auntie Gertie says that when the issue of water came up, she did what she does best—she stirred up the community and called the media.

After a good night's rest, she says, she woke up with a plan. She went to her neighborhood and told the women there to bring everything they needed to do their washing. Then they marched to the civic center where she shouted, "Go inside and use the toilets, and get your children from school."

To gain media attention, the women then hung their worn-out panties and children's underwear on a line outside the civic center. The police soon came, she says, and asked the crowd to stop and vacate the premises.

Auntie Gertie smiles with pride as she remembers her response: "We are going to stay here."

The following day, after the protest made the front pages of Cape Town's leading daily papers and the television news, a fleet of trucks showed up at the settlement with pipes for clean water and toilets.

But victories like this have been few in recent years.

Although the Constitution guarantees access to water for all people, and the ruling African National Congress (ANC) has in its platform a promise of free clean water by 2010, millions are still walking to springs for their daily water or congregating at communal taps.

From 1994, when apartheid was formally dismantled and the ANC won the country's first non-racial elections, to 2002, more than a million South Africans were disconnected from water because they couldn't pay, and 40,000 children died each year from diarrhoea caused by dirty water, according to Ashwin Desai, author of *We Are the Poors.*

The chronic lack of water access in poverty-ridden communities, combined with insufficient free basic water and the high price of water meters, has left many South Africans to ponder the thirteen-year-old Constitution's promise of water access for all.

In Khayelitsha, a black township thirty minutes from the tourist-driven economy of Cape Town, Priscilla Ngandeka lives with her husband and three children. Her "woody" shack, as she calls it, has no running water or toilet. "We are supposed to get water from other sites," she says.

The streets around her home are flooded with dirty water from residents dumping waste into the streets. The smells from the streets are unbearable, adding to the unsanitary living conditions where disease is rampant—conditions that also constitute a significant economic drain on the country, experts say. One study found that the country spent as much as $125 billion each year in direct medical expenses and lost work-time due to water-related diseases.

Still, Ngandeka hopes the government will take action and provide clean water for her neighborhood. "Water, electricity, and toilets are special things for everyone," she says, adding that she thinks the government is doing its best, but that it may need to try a little harder.

Meanwhile, millions are without water, and many of those that are connected struggle to pay the premiums brought on by water privatization, say community activists. Nearly twenty-two million South Africans—half of the country's population—live below the poverty line, with an average income of R144 ($21) a month. The installation of pre-paid water meters—a new development that came with privatization—discriminates against those who cannot afford the prices, which average around R62 ($9) for 2,000 liters, activists say.

With electricity, says Auntie Gertie, you can use candles if you can't afford light, but what can you use instead of water?

The government allots 6,000 liters of free basic water to an eight-person household each month. After a household has used that amount, its members now must pay for additional water through the pre-paid meter system. But this allotment has been challenged in numerous court cases, most recently in 2005 by Peter Gleick, an American environmental scientist.

Gleick brought an affidavit before the city of Johannesburg when his suit came to trial, stating that the government's allotted twenty-five liters per person per day was "insufficient for some basic needs defined by international standards."

He argued that "the amount provided on household units rather than on a per capita daily calculation automatically disadvantages any household of more than eight people. A more appropriate and fair calculation should be based on BWR (Basic Water Requirements) on a per person per day basis."

The official daily ration of twenty-five liters—an amount roughly equivalent to seventy twelve-ounce bottles—is to be used for a person's washing, cleaning, cooking and drinking. But many South Africans who surpass this allotment and cannot afford the price of pre-paid water are seeking other ways to get it, according to members of the growing anti-privatization movement.

Up to 2000, most Kwazulu-Natal residents got their water from communal taps, says Trevor Ngwane, who heads the Soweto Electricity Crisis Committee (SECC) in a township outside Johannesburg. Once pre-paid water meters were installed, however, those who could not afford the premiums took water from a local spring, which happened to be contaminated and triggered a cholera outbreak.

More than twenty people died trying to get free water, says

Ngwane, whose committee is a charter member of the Johannes-burg-based Anti-Privatization Forum (http://www.apf.org.za).

In a region where more than 50 percent of the population is officially unemployed, putting a price on water, a basic necessity, can be devastating, Ngwane says. Those who cannot afford water become angry and try to steal it. Workers often get drunk and kick over the meters and communal taps.

During the past three years, there have been numerous spontaneous community uprisings over water issues with no involvement from trade unions or social movements usually associated with political protests, says Ngwane. Now, he adds, the SECC is trying to unite these communities and expose the government's poor performance.

A key part of the SECC strategy is tapping into the high levels of anger among the people in the overcrowded townships, especially the youth. With more than 70 percent of young black men unemployed and with no resources to attend university or find work, many are becoming frustrated.

However, while many South Africans say the government is not doing enough, some infrastructure for expanded public access to water is now under construction. ANC officials say there have been notable improvements in the delivery of basic services like water and sanitation, citing as an example one township out-side Pretoria, the country's executive capital.

"All communities must have access to clean water and decent sanitation by 2010," according to a January 2007 ANC press release in which the party claims that eight million people out of a targeted thirteen million have already gained access to clean water since the end of apartheid.

Meanwhile, back in Langa, Auntie Gertie rocks back in her chair as the smile fades from her face. Gazing around the empty classroom, she says firmly: "Clean running water is a necessity, not a luxury."

Waiting for housing

By Beth Maclin
Soweto, South Africa

At the entrance to the squatter camp sits a bright green chemical toilet, accented with a gray top and door. A narrow lane winds past it to a collapsing building where three young men lean against two pay phone booths with no phones. The door and windows are gone, and the tin roof protects only half the interior.

The path leads into the heart of a cluster of improvised shelters—called an "informal settlement" in South Africa—where poverty confronts a visitor at every turn. From one shack, a young boy around three years old wanders into the tiny dirt yard amidst a few freshly sprouting weeds. He walks up to the bent chain-link fence and grabs hold, just inches from a twist of barbed wire.

He wears no shoes, despite the fact that it is winter in South Africa. The bottoms of his jeans hover at his heals, barely above the ground. His thin navy-blue and red hoodie is open over a bright blue T-shirt.

During the past few days, plunging temperatures have shattered fifty-four records across the country, according to the *Mail & Guardian*, South Africa's main weekly newspaper. More than fifteen people have died, with nearby Johannesburg, South Africa's largest city, expecting temperatures to drop to freezing.

The boy stands and stares as eleven students from Simmons College snap photographs of him while they shiver under their jackets, sweaters, hats, and socks.

The dirt path, sprinkled with shards of glass and cigarette butts, winds past improvised wood and metal shelters—none with an internal source of heat—deep in the heart of Soweto (South West Township), which was created during the 1890s gold rush to house poorly paid black laborers and is now a magnet for impoverished rural migrants. Yet less than a mile away in Diepkloof, known as the Beverly Hills of Soweto, are gated mansions owned by black families who have risen into the middle and upper classes.

Despite the new Constitution's guarantee of access to housing for all, the stark class disparities in the townships that ring all the country's largest cities reveal the uneven process of remedying the inequalities institutionalized under apartheid, as a small number have benefited from "black empowerment" programs while the vast majority are still waiting their turn.

When the African National Congress (ANC) came to power in South Africa's first democratic elections in 1994, more than 7 million people—almost all of them black—lacked adequate housing, according to the South African Human Rights Commission (SAHRC), itself a product of the new constitution. The ANC pledged to change this.

South Africa's Department of Housing now claims on its Web site that it has built almost 2.4 million houses in the past twelve years. "Our annual production has grown from 252,000 (which in itself was a record we were proud of), to 272,000 (and still counting), for the past year," says Housing Minister Lindiwe Sisulu. "We need to tell this good news it portends a good future for millions still trapped in poverty, and it attests to the fact that the inhospitable firmament is clearing, and there will be better days."

But while most South Africans say there has been progress under the ANC government, some are growing impatient with what they see as the slow pace of housing delivery, and a growing number worry that the promise of universal access to housing will not be met.

"I'm too much of a realist to think that it's possible," says Kim Dennett, a white tour guide. "People have been waiting for five years on a waiting list for housing. People are made promises of being next on the list, and it's broken time and time again."

"I know a lot has been done," she adds, "but it's a drop in the ocean of what is needed." Dennett also criticizes the quality of government-built housing, calling it "rubbish."

Meanwhile, new community organizations are protesting the government's slow progress and pressuring it not only to fulfill the promise of adequate housing but to provide everyone with affordable basic services like electrification and sanitation. The fact that the rickety shacks in Soweto's informal settlements lack such services, while a few blocks away Winnie Mandela's three-story home sits behind a tall brick wall guarded by high-tech surveillance cameras is not lost on these activists.

"South Africa actually is the most unequal society in the world," says Trevor Ngwane, a leader of the Soweto Electricity Crisis Committee, which is one of more than a dozen new protest groups that have banded together in a coalition called the Anti-Privatization Forum.

"There's more inequality now than under apartheid," he says, arguing that apartheid is being de-racialized but not dismantled. "By and large, people are growing poorer, and most resources are being monopolized by fewer and fewer people."

Part of the problem, according to ANC critics, is that apartheid was not just a political system that favored some and discriminated against others—one that could be fixed by taking down the "whites-only" signs and giving everyone the chance to vote. It was also an intricate system of economic exploitation that penetrated all levels of South African society and created self-perpetuating extremes of wealth and poverty.

Communities like Soweto were used as dumping grounds to relocate black, "colored" and Asian South Africans driven out of neighborhoods reserved for whites under the Group Areas Act of 1950. This was part of the National Party's policy of complete racial separation—the essence of apartheid—after it came to power in 1948.

Each of the four racially defined groups was given its own designated place to live. Blacks were further classified according to ethnic origin and assigned citizenship in remote tribal "homelands," which reduced them to the status of temporary migrants while living or working in the cities. But this was not all.

Blacks were shunted into the most difficult and dangerous jobs, from construction to gold-mining, while being paid bare subsistence wages and blocked from organizing themselves, even as the best jobs were officially "reserved" for whites. Much the same was true for education, which was designed to prepare each group for its station in this draconian social experiment.

The continuing impact of these policies and the economic gaps they entrenched is evident on a walk through the Soweto settlement. Along the dirt path, cushioned by overgrown grass and brush, the Simmons students come to a bridge over a small stream. To one side are red shirts, blue jeans, dingy white underwear, and other items hung out to dry in the cold, fall air. More wet clothes are rolled in a ball to the side, awaiting space on the line.

The tour guide, a Sowetan himself, calls this an example of the relationships among the different classes in Soweto: Lower class families wash the clothes of the middle and upper classes to make money. Each group depends upon the other. What he does not say is that this was also true of the symbiotic relationship between whites and blacks throughout apartheid. Now, as then, the contrasts in the living standards produced by this skewed relationship are dramatic.

From the bridge, visitors gazing in one direction look back at a sea of tumbledown shacks, surrounded by overgrown grass, one with the clothesline tied to its side. On the other side of the bridge, within fifty feet, is a prosperous middle class community of paved streets, well-tended lawns, and spacious two-story wood and brick homes.

At one house, Joshua, a pensioner, unlocks the ten-foot high gate to his yard and invites the students to enter. His sits on a stool on his back porch, which is itself more than twice the size of a typical shack. He does not wear a jacket, but keeps warm with a paraffin lamp. He says that a small outbuilding nearby—his summer kitchen—now serves as storage with winter on its way.

Inside the freshly painted, four-room house, which has electricity and running water, the students peer into one of the bedrooms where a woman watches over a sleeping baby, its bare feet sticking out from beneath a soft cotton blanket.

"I was surprised by some of the better areas, like Diepkloof," says Dennett later. "It looks like mine or some of my neighbors. The squatter camps got me the most. You see those shacks and children. I mean, it's cold outside. Imagine living in a shack."

Its insistence that access to housing is a right makes South Africa's Constitution one of the most progressive in the world. It also stokes high expectations among South Africans for what their government should do for them—and when.

While the focus on human rights in the West is often limited to individual civil and political rights, South Africa has embraced a commitment to a broad range of economic, social and cultural rights, from housing to education, health care and a safe environment—what human rights professionals often term second and third generation rights to mark the evolution in the global human rights movement. The difficulty comes in determining how to interpret the government's performance.

Some, like the Soweto Electricity Crisis Committee, say the government has done nowhere near enough. SAHRC chair Jody Kollapen says it is more complicated than simply counting the houses that have been built and the number of people waiting for them because what has been promised is not houses themselves but access.

"When you use the term access, it's wider," he says. "If it was housing, it would suggest that you have the right to housing, and therefore the state has an obligation to make housing available, whether it's now or progressively.

"The right to have access to housing is interpreted as being the right to have an environment that enables you to acquire a house—whether it's a house that's built by the state, whether it's access to a housing subsidy, whether it's access to land. So it's broader in terms of providing the enabling environment for someone to have access to a home, as opposed to limiting it to the right to housing."

Nearly 900 miles to the southwest—just outside Cape Town, the country's legislative capital—lies Langa, one of the oldest black townships in South Africa, as visiting Simmons students learn on a walking tour of the community. Like Soweto, it houses people of radically different social classes where the government is challenged to move people out of informal settlements and into permanent housing.

An empty field is littered with garbage and the remnants of dismantled shacks, torn down to make way for new government-built housing. To one side are the five drab two-story wooden apartment buildings, which look even dingier beneath the dark, rolling clouds that signal an impending storm.

On the other side is a massive, sprawling shack settlement. Two young men stand in the dark in their fifteen-by-ten-foot tin shack. Black garbage bags and pieces of tarp are tacked on the roof and sides to keep the rain from leaking inside. There is no running water.

Meanwhile, only 100 yards to the rear and closer to the heart of Langa, stands an evenly-laid brick road lined with homes that would not seem out of place on the Mediterranean—bright yellow and orange townhouses with late model cars in front of almost every one. The glow of an overhead light spilling over the edges of one window frame reveals a family whose members appear at ease and comfortable.

It is these kinds of stark contrasts, visible to most South Africans on a daily basis, that fuel the growing impatience among the poor for fulfillment of the promise of safe and secure housing for all. But government officials say they may have a long wait.

"The right to access to housing can be realized only subject to the availability of adequate resources. Given the limited funds allocated every year in the budget for this purpose, it will take many years before the housing backlog will be eradicated," says the SAHRC in a recent report.

"Moreover," the report says, "the large number of people who live in informal housing, or who have no access to housing whatsoever, also poses a serious challenge to the state, which is constitutionally obliged to formulate programs taking account of this reality."

Shackdwellers contend with more than cold

By Lucìa Cordón
Khayelitsha, South Africa

Strategically placed pots, cups and plastic containers collect rain-drops that fall through the ceiling. Peach-colored paint drips down the cardboard walls onto the hard-packed dirt floors.

The leaky four-room shack is all Jwana Mfanana, his pregnant sister, her son, and his uncle have for a home, built in less than three days in 2002, after a fire destroyed everything they had. This year, his tragedy was replicated when dozens of people lost their homes—and at least seventeen, their lives—to fire during a record cold snap.

The uneven distribution of electricity in South Africa's rapidly growing squatter camps is leading many shack dwellers to seek alternative heating methods that result in hundreds of deaths each year through the mishandling of open fires inside their ramshackle homes, according to local activists who are disturbed by the phenomenon and organizing to deal with it.

Mfanana's experience is typical.

"No one was working at the time, and we were struggling to even bury my sister,"Mfanana says through a translator on a winter night in June, recalling his loss after the fire took away his sister and his home. "I struggled to go to school, and we only had one bedroom and some few dishes and cups."

Carved, rusty oil drums exhale puffs of smoky burnt wood and coal near many dwellings today. Huddling side by side, families take in the mild warmth that quickly dissipates into the cold night wind. Such unsafe heating systems are common during the icy cold months of May and June.

Mfanana says he remembers coming to Khayelitsha from the impoverished Eastern Cape in 1990, accompanied by his father and his seventeen-year-old sister. On cold nights, the routine was always the same.

"It was five o'clock when they lit up the fire in a metal barrel outside. At eight o'clock they brought the drum into the living room to make themselves warm before going to bed," he says.

Mfanana sits stoically in his battened arm chair, looking at his hands as he recalls the night he awoke to a blazing fire that blocked the path to the door. As he and his father escaped the inferno, he says he realized his sister was still inside. They fought past the flames, which had engulfed the house, but they were too late.

Father and son found themselves with no place to sleep and little hope of recovering what they had lost, he says. His sister died three days later at a nearby hospital.

Meanwhile, unexpected winter weather this year set new temperature records in the major cities, with Johannesburg and Cape Town averaging 37 degrees Fahrenheit. Reports came in from across the country of people dying in fires or freezing to death, even as activists in newly formed advocacy groups stepped up their campaign to pressure the government to make good on its promise of adequate housing for all.

South Africa's Bill of Rights promises everyone the right of access to adequate housing, but the government has not kept up with the growing demand. As hundreds of new homes have been constructed, thousands of impoverished South Africans have moved from the rural areas into the outskirts of major cities. Local activists say that those applying for housing may wait for more fifteen years before getting one.

At the same time, electricity piracy has become common in these rapidly growing shantytowns—termed informal settlements here—where people splice their own connections to passing wires. These hook-ups can result in accidents causing serious injuries and death and, in doing so, graphically illustrating the enormous gap that remains between the haves and have-nots in South Africa, more than a decade after the country's first democratic elections.

"There's more inequality in South Africa now than under apartheid," says Trevor Ngwane, head of the Soweto Electricity Crisis Committee. "Most of the resources are being monopolized by fewer and fewer people."

Individuals are able to purchase fixed amounts of electricity through pre-paid electric meters, he says. But many cannot afford to buy enough electricity to provide heat and lighting for their homes. The committee argues that privatization and the pre-paid electric meter system are the causes for electricity cut-offs and unequal distribution.

It is difficult to separate the issues of housing and electrification from the problem of poverty. At least 48.5 percent of South Africans lived under the poverty line in 2002, according to the National Labour and Economic Development Fund. Most of these families cannot afford to buy enough electricity for heating. Again, Jwana Mfanana's story is typical.

Seven months after his sister's death, Mfanana's father passed away. The twenty-nine-year-old Mfanana, who had returned to school and was in the ninth grade at Sinethemba High in the town of Phillipi, says he was forced to quit in order to seek a job and provide a regular income that would allow him to bury his father and build a new home.

Today, Mfanana works as a construction contractor. His minimal income must support his pregnant elder sister, an uncle and a brother who recently moved into the small shack from the Eastern Cape, he says, as the three sit around him somberly listening as he recalls the tragedy.

"Now we are scared of doing the fire again, so we are using a paraffin stove—a small one—so when we are getting cold, we will just light it, and then we will sit by it. Then we will switch it off, and we will go to bed," says Mfanana.

The installation of low-capacity fuse boxes in most poor households makes it impossible to use energy-intensive appliances, according to a 2000 South African Human Rights Commission report. "The fuse box can be replaced for a relatively modest sum, but it appears many families are not aware of this fact," the report says.

As a result, many still use open fires or pirated connections, often with dire consequences. More than seventeen fire-caused deaths were reported in Johannesburg alone after the May 24 cold snap.

Though a government-sponsored initiative to prevent fires proposed an educational workshop that focuses on children who might be victims of fire accidents during the winter.

Colorful scenes depicting children's rights are sown into a mural in the Junior Education Center of Constitution Hill, part of a national museum linked to the constitutional court in

Johannesburg. Fifty-five children from different informal settlements are chosen during the winter to participate in the fire prevention workshop.

"Kids, when they are by themselves at home, their parents are at work. When it's wintertime, it's getting darker earlier so they try to light a candle, but they forget when they light a candle; you find they forget and start to play. The candle isn't looked after and there is a fire in the house," says Z.B. Nkabinde, a worker at the site.

This year, black children from Freedom Park, white children from White Ridge in Newlands and Indian and "colored" children from Denver (a Johannesburg suburb) are invited to the workshop with their parents. Transportation is also provided by the center to ensure children's opportunity to attend.

The Bill of Rights commits that the government is committed to providing basic services for all. Last year, Parliament passed the Electricity Regulation Amendment bill, which requires the government to extend electricity services to all municipalities.

Yet millions of people remain without electricity today, according to the South Africa Development Fund, a Boston-based charity that has been working with communities in South Africa for more than twenty years.

South Africans are not prepared for these climate conditions and if the government is not able to provide the necessary services, individuals are forced to find alternative methods, which can be many times harmful to themselves and their families.

Organizations such as the Soweto Electricity Crisis Committee, the Anti-Eviction Campaign, the Anti-Privatization Forum and the Orange Farm Water Crisis Committee work on a local level fighting for peoples right to basic services. They represent people living in informal settlements who do not have a voice.

Meanwhile, Mfanana tries to rebuild his home and family, though he says it will take years of work and struggle.

"Ever since the accident happened, you can look around. There's nothing right. If you want to look around, you can look around," says Mfanana.

"There's nothing right," he repeats.

New houses are not enough

By Paula Bettencourt
Cape Town, South Africa

Low lights cover the walls softly, creating an atmosphere of quiet. Hand-drawn lines, in bright colors crisscross the floor, detailing streets and places that defined a long-gone community.

Picture by picture, the walls give face to a lost people. Panel by panel their stories are told. In the back, a woman sits alone stitching letters and numbers with deep purple thread upon pure white cloth.

"People are dying before they can come home," says Menisha Collins, the seamstress at the District Six Museum in Cape Town. She is a former resident of District Six herself, forcibly evicted with her family under an apartheid-era ethnic cleansing policy known as "black spot removal" when she was a young girl. Now, she volunteers as a motivational speaker for the former residents when they visit the museum. Meanwhile, she stitches the names and messages of visitors into panels that become part of the exhibit.

Since the forced removal in the 1960s, the infrastructure of District Six has been completely demolished. Most of the area remains an empty field near the port city's bustling industrial center. The current government of the African National Congress (ANC) has promised the restoration of District Six, but so far only a handful of families has been able to move back in.

The legacy of apartheid has left communities like District Six broken and thousands of non-whites without permanent homes, creating a housing crisis that is exacerbated by rapid urban population growth.

This growth comes from a continual influx of people from the poorer rural areas to the city looking for jobs and better living conditions. Yet poverty affects the city, too, and it threatens the stability of communities both old and new.

These factors diminish the government's ability to build the homes promised in the urban areas under the country's 1996 Constitution, and, after twelve years of the "New South Africa," a sense of crisis still pervades many black and "colored" communities, instead of security.

When the diverse community of District Six was dismantled, it was divided along racial lines, and people were placed into townships according to the apartheid state's racial designations— European, Asian, "colored" (mixed race) and African. Those residents with the economic means were able to move into decent homes and buy property, but the mostly black majority was forced out of their houses and into informal settlements.

Such forced divisions happened across South Africa after the far right National Party (NP) came to power in 1948 and imposed the draconian system of racial domination known as apartheid (Afrikans for separateness). The NP government, some of whose leaders had supported the Nazis in World War II, criminalized interracial coupling and marriages, as well as racially mixed households. This split up families and communities.

Once all the racial groups were separated and relocated from District Six, the buildings and structures were destroyed. This meant that new housing would have to be constructed on top of the old homes, but disputes over this held up such redevelopment, and the area remained vacant for decades.

Apartheid finally ended in 1994 when the ANC came to power in the first multi-racial national elections in South Africa's history. Two years later, a constitution was ratified that guaranteed everyone not only political rights under the law but also economic, social and cultural rights. In doing so, South Africans sought to rectify the wrongs of the past.

Among other things, the post-apartheid constitution guaranteed a right of access to adequate housing. The national parliament went on to pass a law committing the state to build one million houses every five years throughout the country. However, according to Human Rights Commission chair Jody Kollapen, fewer than two million houses have actually been built in the decade since then.

These new homes go to people living in temporary homes who are waiting upon a very long waitlist, Kollapen says. However, once the permanent homes are received, they are difficult to hold on to.

Gertrude Square, an activist with the Western Cape Anti-Eviction Campaign in Valhalla Park outside Cape Town, fought the government three times to keep from being evicted, and she has continued to fight for others in her community as well. These evictions arise because people cannot both pay their rent and cover the cost of basic necessities for their families, she says.

Square's housing problems began with her inability to pay rent, due to the cost of transportation to her job and the need to buy food and pay school fees for her children on her modest income, she says. This resulted in her being evicted, which she avoided at first by borrowing money from others to pay back the municipality that manages much of the rental housing in black and "colored" townships now, much as it did during apartheid.

Square says that after the third time she was evicted, she worked with government officials to understand the poverty element to the housing issue, and her rent was finally reduced. Aware that she was not the only one in this situation, she says she helped found the Anti-Eviction Campaign for her community as part of a rapidly growing new activist movement that is challenging the ANC government to follow through on its promise to end apartheid not only in politics but throughout the wider society.

Her fight with the government did not stop with fighting eviction from the homes in Valhalla Park. Square says that after years of waiting for more homes to be built on land that was undeveloped and getting the answer that the government did not have the money to build houses, the community came together in 2003 to build an informal settlement on its own. But the government responded with force.

"They came with the whole police force and the army. They demolished the structures and shot rubber bullets and beat us," says Square.

After the government secured a court order to demolish the new settlement, the community went to court to fight for approval to build on the land, and after three years, she says, they won.

The second fight over the informal settlement was to get water and water facilities to the families living in this settlement. The newly built informal homes had no access to running water, and residents were using untested and possibly harmful water for all their needs, she says. After being told that the government was not required to install pipes, the group took action again.

With panties in hand, Square says she led the women to do their washing by using the local civic center's water facilities. The government and media arrived when their panties were line-drying out in the open. Their victory came soon afterward.

"Clean running water is a necessity, not a luxury," says Square decisively. But her concerns do not stop there.

The Constitution guarantees access to "adequate housing" not just houses, Square points out. This may include clean running water, four walls and a roof, but for many it is more than that. A person without access to jobs or transportation can easily lose access to a house since the house itself is not guaranteed.

Most informal settlements are close to the industrial centers where much of the employment is, so transportation costs from there are lower than from outlying government-sanctioned developments. Some settlement residents can even walk to their jobs, she says. But new construction often occurs farther away, and, like many of those now in Valhalla Park, potential residents often do not want to move there, even though they are eager to get new houses.

"They do not want to move out of the homes they built, for without their jobs they won't be able to keep the new houses anyway," Square says. Nor do they want to lose the community ties they have built up where they are now.

But these improvised communities are not the only ones threatened by post-apartheid developments. Bo-Kapp, a centuries-old Malay community in the heart of Cape Town, is also fighting for its survival, according to community activist Shereen Habib, who says the problem there is not the government but newly unleashed market forces.

Bo-Kapp sits on a lush, scenic mountainside that rises behind the city center and provides spectacular views of both the coastline and the looming bulk of Table Mountain. Skilled slaves that Dutch colonists brought to Cape Town from what is now Indonesia, India, and elsewhere in Asia and the Pacific built the homes themselves. But this is not all that makes this community significant.

Bo-Kapp was one of the only mixed racial communities that survived the policies of apartheid. Its infrastructure and history were saved from demolition through the united efforts of residents and sympathizers who challenged the government on historical grounds. But the community is now under threat from another source.

"What apartheid could not do, globalization is doing now,"

Shereen Habib says softly, as she looks out to the horizon. There is not just anger in her voice, but anguish, too. She says that since South Africa became a true democracy, rich South Africans and foreigners seeking holiday getaways have been buying up homes and land that had been passed down from one generation to the next. Now, these new economic forces are dispersing the community.

"They become summer homes—the people do not live in them," says Habib. But residents are coming together here, much as in Valhalla Park, to defend themselves against this threat to their community.

Some were selling their houses because the area is prime real estate, says Habib. They were being offered huge payments that they could use to help their struggling families. But once the community began organizing itself and educating its members on the impact this had on their unique heritage, much of the sell-off stopped. Nevertheless, it is still a fight, she adds.

When Habib recently went to an elderly woman's house to visit, she says the woman told her that her property taxes had increased again and again as the property values went up. But her income, minimal as it as, stayed the same.

"People are finding it harder and harder to pay the rates," Habib says. To combat this new threat, she says she is working to bring even more tourism to the area to add income for residents and help them balance the rising costs of living—all to preserve the integrity of her community.

Across the city, Menisha Collins works to put District Six back together by pushing the government to keep its promise of restoration. "There are plans in the works right now," she says, as the long panel on restitution hangs to her left in the museum.

To Collins, the empty field where District Six once stood needs to be filled with houses and the families that used to live there sooner rather than later. Many people are waiting in shacks for these new homes in the place of their old ones, she says. But, she adds, all miss their old community and need it back to put their own lives in order and to let go of the pain and anger from the past once and for all.

"We were rich in spirit of the community," Collins says softly with tears in her eyes. "We were poor, but we were happy."

Visitors to the Constitutional Court, whose walls are made of bricks from one of Johannesburg's most notorious political prisons, enter through a gallery of contemporary art with a towering ladder whose steps represent the ordeals the South African people went through to achieve their freedom. (Debbie Hird/The Image Works)

Though Johannesburg's political prison was dismantled to make way for the Constitutional Court, several towers were left standing. (Dan Connell/The Image Works)

Mahatma Ghandi developed his commitment to non-violence during his 21 years in South Africa, part of it in the Johannesburg prison. (Dan Connell/The Image Works)

The Constitution Hill Museum teaches visitors the meaning of human rights. (Dan Connell/The Image Works)

Eritrean exiles promote democracy and human rights in their homeland. (Dan Connell/The Image Works)

A Soweto child peers at Simmons reporters as they pass through his "informal settlement." (Dan Connell/The Image Works)

Khayelitsha residents go to great lengths to decorate homes and schools despite chronic poverty. (Dan Connell/The Image Works)

Anti-apartheid-activist-turned-tour-guide Shereen Habib scans a book by another Simmons group. (Dan Connell/The Image Works)

Students try Malay food in Cape Town's historic Bo-Kaap quarter, now threatened by gentrification. (Dan Connell/The Image Works)

Cape Town's District Six Museum preserves the symbols of the apartheid era. (Beth Maclin)

Cape Town's District Six Museum charts the history of repression during the apartheid era. (Beth Maclin)

Cape Town's historic Slave Lodge displays the instruments of oppression. (Dan Connell/The Image Works)

Cape Town health workers demand higher wages and more support for public health. (Dan Connell/The Image Works)

Children locked out of school by a teachers' strike join parents in a Khayelitsha protest. (Dan Connell/The Image Works)

Social Rights:
Education

Get-rich-quick mentality dominates urban youth

By Lucìa Cordón
Manenberg, South Africa

Three fingertips are barely visible under a generous stack of bills.

The rest of the hand is concealed.

Beneath the black and white picture on the cover of the pamphlet are the words, "Why money?"

At the foot of the page, several horizontal lines are left blank for a response.

This is the first thing street-wise, young South Africans see when they pick up this home-made packet of educational materials designed to wean them from a life of gangs, drugs and violence.

The money gets their attention.

"Other programs before were written, and the kids were illiterate and didn't understand the words. They would get angry because they could not read, so I decided to use pictures. A picture tells a lot of words, and when they see the pictures, they identify," says Magadien Wentzel, the creator of the package.

More than a decade after the racist apartheid system was abolished, a get-rich-quick mentality appears to dominate among South Africa's urban youth. Many seek shortcuts to succeed in their communities where only a few are able to flourish through legitimate channels.

Equal opportunity and protection of the individual are key principles in South Africa's Bill of Rights. However, many young "colored" and black South Africans struggle to protect their dignity in the economically segmented country.

The unemployment rate nearly doubled from 1995 to 2002, rising from 16 percent to 30.5 percent, according to a recent Human Rights Commission report. Today, experts estimate that the unemployment rate for people under the age of thirty is around 70 percent.

Former gang leader Magadien Wentzel is trying to change that.

Four years after his release from a twenty-five-year prison

sentence, Wentzel writes pamphlets and offers workshops for youths at risk. His most recent program is titled "The Other Side of the Coin." Once a prominent high-ranking official of the "colored" 28 gang, he says he knows all the dangers the underprivileged youth of the Cape Flats face.

An Easy Ticket

"I grew up in an apartheid system where I had to do everything in my power to become successful," says Wentzel. "There were different curriculums for everyone: The blacks must become my boys, and I should become the white man's boy."

He says he remembers the frustration he felt knowing he could not become a qualified lawyer even after passing his exams with honors. The most he could hope for was to become a clerk to a white lawyer. A black man's success meant becoming an office assistant, although he would most likely end up working as a cleaner.

"When I joined the gang, I could make maneuvers. I could find ways to fight the system. I could get anything I wanted: drugs, power, money and protection. If I wanted a room in an expensive hotel for a month, the gang would pay for it for a year," says Wentzel.

With this lack of opportunity in South Africa today, youth unemployment is a serious concern. "A high percent of the youth are not working. It means that youth aren't qualified so they can't find a job, or it's youth that have the qualifications but just can't get a job. They are really frustrated," says Trevor Ngwane, head of the Soweto Electricity Crisis Committee and leader of his community.

A black student at the University of Cape Town, Patrick Bashala considers himself fortunate to have the opportunity of a higher education. "There is a lot of pressure. Especially in a country like South Africa where the high percentage of unemployment is a constant reminder of the hardship of not having a job," he says.

Government Campaigning

In 1998 the South African government introduced the Employment Equity Act. This system of affirmative action forced employers to develop employment equity plans to support black employees.

Five years later, the Black Employment Equity Act was passed, which was intended to promote black ownership and black management by awarding companies that held black individuals in these positions. The government publicly backed sectors that adopted the code.

Although the number of black employees in management branches increased, nearly 50 percent of all senior management and professional positions were still held by white employees, according to a StatsSA labour force survey in 2002. Black South African's account for 79.5 percent of the country's population while whites are only 9.2 percent, according to a 2006 Stats SA report.

Many privileged "colored" and black professionals in high-ranking posts appear to be content with just finding prestigious positions for themselves. Some are unsympathetic to the large unemployed population since the problem does not affect them directly. "If you are able to find a good job, you are not exposed to the issues of unemployment and poverty. You know, but you don't want to know," says Bashala.

The increase of blacks in high corporate positions has little effect on the black majority, most of whom remain extremely poor. These positions demand qualifications that require high levels of education and experience, which are still available to a relatively small number of people.

"If you are able to get a management degree, it is easier for you to get a job. But most jobs require experience, and you've just come out from school with little or no work experience," says Bashala.

The biggest obstacle faced by young people coming from poor areas is their inability to further their education. Many young impoverished black and "colored" South Africans who struggle to finish elementary school and are unable to continue with higher education see gangs as a solution for acquiring wealth and power, according to Wentzel.

"Gangs, you find them in every corner. Just like churches. You can't run away from drugs, you can't run away from gangsterism. It's choices that you have to make and be very strong," says Wentzel.

A 2003 government report on education showed that 71 percent of the population over twenty years old did not have a secondary education.

"If you look at gangs, you find that there are no stupid kids. You find that more than 50 percent of the gang members are matriculates. Their parents can't afford to send them to a college or a technicon," says Wentzel, referring to post-secondary vocational schools.

Designer Culture

"That is where it ends. They end matric, they join the gangs, and the gang gives them work selling drugs and sex, and in return they get protection," Wentzel says.

Gang members, drug addicts and school dropouts are the people Wentzel counsels. They hear about millionaire drug lords and dream about moving to posh areas like Constantia, Durbanville, and Bellville.

Diesel, Billabong, Levis, and Caterpillar. "Young people love name tags. If it comes out today, you find it in the Cape Flats. Where do they steal it? Where do they buy it? I don't know, but you'll find it there," says Wentzel.

Globalization and communication media have changed the way young South Africans see their future.

Clever Kids, West Siders, Born Free Kids, The Gigolos and The Americans—these are the names for gangs in the Cape Flats. The Americans wear American designer clothes, American designer jewelry. After September 11, members of the gang cried and held up the United States flag after September 11, says Wentzel.

"They don't want to be South Africans: They want to be African Americans. It's not because they are stupid. They see the TV and how people in the U.S. have money. It's something that they long for," he says.

Bashala says that young people's priorities have changed. There is more competition among college students to succeed. However, it upsets him to see how these hard working students ignore the problems underprivileged South Africans face. "People live in a bubble. If you can drive a nice car and are able to go home to your family, you don't care," he adds.

This growing political apathy among youth people is reflected in the poor turnout in elections since the end of apartheid. Less than half of those in the 18-25 age group voted in 2004 when both the presidency and the entire parliament were on the ballot.

"Young people are not interested in politics. Most of them don't even know who politicians are. They don't see the government offering them employment opportunities and if they are hungry and have no place to sleep, the last thing they think about is politics," Wentzel says.

But the roots of the problem are in the conditions they face growing up . "The period between adolescence and adulthood doesn't exist anymore. Sometimes I worry that one of these days, we won't have a youth. They are using too much drugs, getting angry and violent. They don't care who they kill anymore, as long as they kill," he says.

Ex-Gangster as Santa Claus

Wentzel contemplates the newspaper clipping for a moment. Then he holds it up with amusement as he points at a picture of himself wearing a red and white Santa Claus hat. "Last year I gave 200 children Christmas presents. I want to teach them there is a life better than drugs. Teach them about education and choices," he says.

Two years ago Wentzel started a youth group with fifteen members from the ages of fourteen to twenty-six years. "If you are young you are still welcome," he says. Last year he fundraised to send twenty-two young people to the Technicon University of Cape Town. There they learned basic sewing, woodwork skills, computer literacy, and communication skills.

Today, his youth group includes forty-five recovering youths. "I don't have any certificates or diplomas or degrees, but I have wisdom and knowledge and I have experience. I like to speak about what is really happening," he says adding that a lot of people call him and ask him to speak to their children.

Wentzel says he is now looking for a college that will give free computer literacy courses to their mothers. "I can teach the kids, but when they go home the parents don't understand. They get frustrated when the kids become more clever than them," he says. And he wants parents to understand what their children are doing and to support them.

In Wentzel's view, people only see one side of the coin—"the designer clothes, the beautiful girls."

"I am trying to teach them that there are two sides to a coin," he says, as he stuffs the newspaper clippings and pamphlets back into his slim business suitcase. "Yes, that is basically what I'm doing, trying to make the world a better place—one day at a time."

Helping street kids:
Small NGOs do it better

By Erika Fields
Cape Town, South Africa

From the outside, the house looks plain and simple. Inside, the walls are painted bright shades of orange and pink. Each bedroom has six or more bunk beds. Nothing is out of place—the beds are all made and there is nothing on the floors.

Twenty-five girls are crowded into these rooms, though there are only sixteen beds. The youngest is two years old, the oldest is nearly eighteen. They come here, often after running away from home, to find sanctuary at Ons Plek (Our Place).

Established in 1988, Ons Plek is the only shelter available to them in Cape Town—open twenty-four hours a day to young street girls who need accommodation, counseling and education. This, along with helping the girls with the complex family reunification process, is the key to the shelter's success, according to Ons Plek publications, which also say that 100-150 girls between the ages of six and eighteen check themselves into the shelter each year to escape physical abuse or neglect—or simply because their families can no longer support them.

"The shelter facility allows the family, child and staff to work together thoroughly," says Deputy Director René Rossouw. "We make arrangements and solve problems together, knowing that the child is safe, and fully cared for under adult guidance.

"In addition to weaning children from street life, the two other crucial focus areas of the project are resettling children in community and vocational preparation. All programs are integrated very closely with each other to equip and prepare the children for their future lives."

They run away from home, find out the shelter is available, and then admit themselves, says Ons Plek Director Pam Jackson. The organization's job is to find out if the girls come there for a good reason, not just because there is hot water and a TV.

Shelter investigations to find out why the girls left home once took weeks, but now they take only days or hours, says Jackson. The girls know that the counselors are not going to force them to go back to abuse at home, so they have become more comfortable telling the truth right away.

Shelter critics say they are too costly and that all they do is institutionalize children without empowering or disciplining them. However, critics of the government, which also runs programs for street children, say that small, independent organizations like Ons Plek are doing a much more efficient job than the state, as they are out in the communities where the children live, while the government is not.

"In the current situation, shelters can be more effective in preventing children from becoming street children and in intervening to change their lives on a permanent basis than any other service," says Jackson. "As a director of an urban shelter for the past twelve years, I agree with many of the criticisms of shelters. It depends on how the shelter is run as to whether these criticisms can be avoided."

The foundation work lies in the shelters, says Jackson. The shelter facility allows the family, the child, and staff to work together thoroughly. Ons Plek workers make arrangements and solve problems together, knowing that the child is safe and fully cared for under adult guidance.

"The reality in South Africa today is that for an NGO with small resources, more effective preventative work can be done using a shelter. In the future, as AIDS orphans fall through the cracks in community safety nets and run to central business districts, shelters may be their only hope to being re-routed back into a community," Jackson says.

There is a lot of communication between the groups that work with street children and the government, says Allerease Olanrewaju, a counselor and community worker at Ons Plek. "But it's a matter of coming down to our level."

South Africa's Bill of Rights guarantees that "every child has the right to be protected from maltreatment, neglect, abuse or degradation." And that is what Ons Plek says it is doing.

"The kids know [their rights]; we tell them all the time," says Jackson, who says she wants the Constitution to be rewritten with not only the rights but the responsibilities that come with them.

"We prevent them from being abused until they can protect

themselves," Jackson says.

These girls' families are poor, she says. Keeping six girls in one bedroom is what they are accustomed, so when they leave Ons Plek, they can go back to their old lives without experiencing a sense of loss from a more comfortable living situation.

The girls also do grocery shopping, take public transportation anywhere they need to go, and do all the house cleaning, so when they leave, they are not far removed from what they will find in the wider society and in their homes, she adds.

Ons Plek staff members say they take pride in empowering the girls to cope with daily life by instilling a sense of responsibility in them. One of the ways they do this is by making the shelter as much like an ordinary household as possible. One measure of their success is that most girls are returned home to their families or put with another family member after just two months at the shelter. Another is the declining number of girls on the streets.

According to Ons Plek, when the shelter opened in 1988, there were approximately sixty girls there who had been on the streets for more than three years, due to the lack of girls' shelters. These numbers increased over the next three years to more than 120.

But just five years later, the number of girls who had been living on the street for more than three years dropped to only seven. But returning the girls to their families and keeping them off the street is not the only way Ons Plek measures its performance.

An example of another kind is provided by "Casey," says Jackson, who asked that the girl's real name be withheld.

Casey had been on the street for three years and was just sixteen years old when she came to Ons Plek. Her confidence was nonexistent, she shook nervously all the time, and she would wet her bed in her sleep, says Jackson. Ons Plek workers thought that school was not an option, as she only had a third grade education. So they decided to keep her at the house, observing her in art therapy.

Casey began to draw pictures of boats, Jackson says. Her early drawings were similar to those of a small child, but the colors were dark.

A few months into art therapy and after being given more and more responsibility around the house, the drawings began to change. After just six months at Ons Plek, they became brighter, as her view of the world changed from negative to positive, says Jackson.

"Were we successful? Yes, in our terms," she says. The aim is to help the child and know what the child can or can not receive. Meanwhile, the local government is taking a different approach.

The city of Cape Town adopted a new law to deal with street children in 2006 titled the "City Streets, Public Places and Public Nuisance Act." This law "not only adds to the vulnerability of the homeless, especially street children, by dispersing them to outlying locations around the city where there are no support mechanicisms, but may also lead to the criminalisation of poverty and homelessness in South Africa," says Bronwen Dyke, writing for the Cape Town magazine *The Big Issue South Africa*.

"Perhaps none are more vulnerable than the children who call the streets of Cape Town home. These children are misunderstood and mistrusted by the general public," says Dyke.

The government is picking up kids on the streets and dropping them off at various centers, says Olanrewaju. But the kids have figured out that by dressing differently, they will not be regarded as street kids. This, he says, is not solving the problem.

"The government is spending a lot of wasted money on this," she says. Meanwhile, groups like Ons Plek are already working to get the kids off the street—and doing so far more effectively.

"We see it as a waste," she says. "We are already existing and doing the work."

Who they are is the question—not where

By Faythe Mallinger
Cape Town, South Africa

Not a single room is empty.

Pam Jackson walks down the staircase that faces the door, looking around for a quiet space. "You just have to shut yourself off from what is happening," she says of the overcrowded home.

Jackson is the director of Ons Plek, an intake shelter for female street children in Cape Town. Established in 1988, the organization is the only intake center for the girls on the streets in Cape Town. Its location amidst colorful old homes in the Woodstock neighborhood, a central area of the city's core, allows youth to easily access the shelter's services.

The clicks of Xhosa conversation, one of South Africa's eleven official languages, echo from room to room. To the right of the foyer sits a teenage girl eating and watching the director greet her visitors. The long, narrow room is filled with four small tables pushed together to accommodate the shelter's twenty-five resident children.

The kitchen lies on the other side of the stairs. Colorful clothes of all sizes hang drying above the washing machine. The girls are responsible for household duties, including washing clothes, cooking, and shopping for food. "We're trying to be very much like the community," says Jackson.

A room with two beds, one occupied by a young girl able to sleep despite the animated exchanges among her housemates, lies adjacent to the foyer.

"Sorry it is messy," says the teenage girl who had been eating in the other room. She is summoned by the director to give visitors a tour of the home.

At the top of the stairs is a small window surrounded by orange walls. Clothing hangs from the stair railing. The girl-guide reminds visitors that residents are responsible for cleaning the home.

Two bedrooms with crowded bunk beds and lockers are separated by the shelter's office. There are sixteen beds in the home, but with extra mattresses the shelter can accommodate up to twenty-five girls.

Ons Plek, "Our Place" in Afrikaans, is one community organization's response to the government's perceived inability to protect the rights of Cape Town's children.

Each year almost 150 girls between six and eighteen years of age leave home to fend for themselves on the streets of Cape Town, according to Ons Plek publications, which charge that these girls—only 2 percent of the children on Cape Town streets—are often ignored or not served by projects set up for street children.

The shelter serves as a frontline defense for the protection of children's rights, organizers say. During the apartheid era, black South Africans were faced with institutionalized oppression and exploitation. Their status throughout the country left them without rights recognized by the state—and African children fared the worst.

At the end of the 1980s the apartheid system began to fall apart under pressure from public protests and international sanctions. The country had its first fully democratic election in 1994 and by 1996 had adopted a new constitution. Section 28 in the new Bill of Rights is dedicated to the rights of the child.

In addition to the guarantee of specific services such as nutrition, shelter, basic health care, and the promise of protection from abuse, neglect, and exploitative labor practices, the Constitution states that: "A child's best interests are of paramount importance in every matter concerning the child."

But this sweeping guarantee has not yet been extended in practice to the approximately 250,000 children now living on South African streets, according to a 2004 estimate by the Consortium for Street Children.

"The only meal of which Mudau can be certain is the one served at midday at Hillbrow's Twilight Children shelter," writes Jeremy Gordin, describing a Johannesburg street child in *The Sunday Independent*. "The only dietary supplements he knows of are tik (crystal methamphetamine), thai white (a cheap heroin derivative, often cut with rat poison) or, best and cheapest of all, good old glue, which on the coldest nights apparently makes one 'feel warm inside.'"

Government officials acknowledge the need for intervention on behalf of these children and say they are working on initiatives to eliminate the problem of child homelessness, though many children's advocates say the state is either not doing enough or doing the wrong things.

"The City of Cape Town, working hand in hand with key stakeholders such as the Provincial Government and the NGO community had succeeded in galvanizing the broader community and bringing even sharper focus on the plight of street children," said Cape Town mayor Nomaindia Mfeketo at the February 2005 launch of a new Integrated Multi-Sectoral Street Children Initiative.

Nicknamed the "Smile-A-Child" campaign, the initiative seeks to raise public awareness about the problem, provide outreach programs and referrals, and employ initiatives toward placement or family reunification by pairing with community organizations, according to its organizers.

Such collaborative work contrasts sharply with campaigns to clean up the streets of other South African cities ahead of the 2010 World Cup—which is expected to draw millions of visitors and will be held in stadiums across the country—by rounding up homeless children and placing them in centers that critics say will serve as holding tanks rather than as rehabilitation facilities.

"Every time we have an occasion in the city, out comes the glitter and the children disappear," Durban city councilor Avrille Coen recently told *The Daily News*. "But, of course, a few days later they manage to find their way back."

Although Cape Town's campaign is a much-needed alternative to other clean-up initiatives and seems designed to reach similar goals to those of Ons Plek, the shelter's organizers say the two differ in their measures of success.

"The government is unrealistic in terms of what it expects people to do," says former Ons Plek resident and volunteer Allerease Olanrewaju. "We do it the proper way."

The government's plan is meant to get children off the streets, she says. Accomplishment means no more street children. But Ons Plek has a different sort of success story, aimed less at where the children are than at who they are and how they behave.

Jackson says she remembers a sixteen-year-old girl who came to the shelter. She had spent three years on the streets prior to her stay at Ons Plek and had only reached grade three in school. She had no confidence, shook nervously all the time, wet the bed every night, and constantly put up a fight.

During her time at the shelter, Jackson says, the girl gradually transformed from aggressive to assertive, and the colors of her artwork got much brighter after six months in art therapy.

"Her worldview had changed," says Jackson.

Throughout the course of her stay, the girl would continue to spend time on the streets. "The street was really [her] world," says Jackson, smiling. Even after leaving Ons Plek, the girl left to live on the streets with her friends and to work odd jobs.

Still, Jackson says this was one of the shelter's most inspiring success stories. In her view, they were successful not in terms of how the world might measure it in statistical terms, but from the child's standpoint and in terms of how she herself was changed.

They give what they can, but they also try to accept the limits to what the child can receive, she says. "If we can do just that, that's something."

For street girls, success is relative

By Kristin Pitts
Cape Town, South Africa

The tour is short because it has to be.

There is a kitchen in the back, where industrial-sized dishes fill open-air cabinets. To the right of the front door is the living room, where unmade cots serve as couches. Up the stairs are two bedrooms, one with six bunk beds, the other with eleven.

Pam Jackson, the shelter's director, sits in an office between the two bedrooms. She apologizes for the lack of space, saying that Ons Plek's other location burned down. Now, she adds, girls who had filled both houses have moved into one, making the two story home feel even smaller than before, when it was already at maximum capacity.

But the real reason for the crowding, Jackson says, is that in Cape Town, where sexual and physical abuse are on the rise, young girls have a lot to run away from.

Ons Plek, a shelter for street girls whose name means "our place" in Afrikaans, fulfills a unique purpose for girls who were running away from danger, only to find themselves in an equal amount of it when confronted by the realities of life on the streets.

"The girls here could go somewhere, and they could go nowhere," Jackson says, shrugging. But her shrug is not one of detachment—it is one that comes from years of experience, and years of trying to find a definition for something hard to place.

So with paperwork piled around her, and a frozen dinner pushed off to the side, Jackson sits in a black padded chair to talk about a term she and her staff have attempted again and again to determine: success.

"I'll tell a story," she says, and settles in among the books and mis-matched chairs.

"Sylvia was sixteen years old; she'd been on the street for three years. When we took her in, she had no confidence. She shook nervously and wet the bed every night," she says.

"We couldn't send her to school. She had only completed grade three," Jackson says.

An intregal part of Ons Plek's policy is flexibility. After nearly twenty years of working with street girls, the Ons Plek staff has found that rigid rules and expectations do not mesh well with children used to life on the streets, where the only thing they can regularly expect is the unexpected. "We kept her at home with the house mom all day, doing some drawing," says Jackson. "She used to draw boats in dark colors."

Just below her, on the first floor, a house mom sits with Ons Plek's youngest member, a two year old. Nearly all the girls here go through art therapy, a technique Jackson admits some find outdated. But its universality, and its popularity with the girls, keep crayons moving and paint flowing.

"After two years she was wetting the bed once every two weeks, and she'd gone through an aggressive stage and moved to an assertive stage," Jackson says. "The colors of her boats got brighter and brighter."

"We got her a job, but she didn't want it. The street was her life, but she had confidence now and wasn't bullied," she says.

As she speaks, the outside world finds its way in through her office window. There are the typical city sounds—cars honking, people talking, cell phones ringing—but most noticeable are the boys. Some are doing manual labor in the lot across from Ons Plek. Others stare silently at the brightly colored building as they walk by. Many sit socializing, just outside the white gates. Jackson notes, with a frown, that their presence is hard to deal with, but perhaps necessary as the Ons Plek staff attempts to prepare girls for the real world.

That preparation—and its outcome—varies greatly from girl to girl. Oftentimes the best way to chart progress is to look at the girl's "life story," a book that contains, either in words or pictures, the girl's life so far. The books, of which there are many on display here, are meant to show not only the girls' past, but their potential for a future.

After their time at Ons Plek is up, girls go on to do a number of things. Some work as cashiers. Some become homeowners. And some, like Sylvia, go back to the streets.

"Were we successful?" Jackson asks, thinking about Sylvia, as a pensive look clouds her face. "No, in terms of how the world sees it, but yes, in how we see it."

Social Rights:
Health Care

Fighting the twin demons of HIV and rape

By Victoria Latto
Khayelitsha, South Africa

Outside a courthouse in this Western Cape township, women hold up signs with handwritten messages emblazoned on them in black marker.

"No bail for rapists, murderers," says one.

"Rapists deserve to die," reads another.

"Nandipha's spirit will always rest in peace," says a third.

The group of fifty adults and children is singing songs of protest and solidarity. Their faces are etched with anger and determination. They say they will stay here as long as necessary.

The demonstrators are demanding justice for eighteen-year-old Nandipha, who was recently gang-raped and killed in Khayelitsha, her body left in a public toilet.

Nandipha was an activist with the Treatment Action Campaign (TAC), a nongovernmental organization (NGO) formed in 1998 to deal with the massive problem of HIV/AIDS in Khayelitsha and elsewhere in the country.

"We just want the government to see that this is not right," says Fumana Ntlontlo, a counselor with TAC. "The community is tired."

Her community has a lot to be tired of. In South Africa, HIV/AIDS and rape are twin epidemics, with some of the world's highest rates of each. According to the Joint United Nations Program on HIV/AIDS (UNAIDS), between 15 percent and 20 percent of South Africans—about 5.5 million people—are HIV positive.

This number is approximately 2.5 times higher for women than men.

A South African woman is raped every six seconds, according to the Triangle Project, a Western Cape NGO focused on gay, lesbian, bisexual, and transgender issues. Since many rapes go unreported, it is difficult to obtain exact statistics. However, TAC and other organizations argue that gender-based violence is one of the highest causes of the spread of HIV.

Nandipha's murder mirrors that of Lorna Mlofana, another young Khayelitsha woman who volunteered at TAC and who was killed five years ago. Mlofana, who was HIV positive, disclosed her status after being gang-raped. She was then killed by her rapists, with little response from police.

It is a scenario all-too-familiar for TAC's Ntlontlo.

"Justice is failing some of us," she says, pointing to the long delays in getting trials, rapists and killers getting out on bail, and jail sentences for rapists being reduced to only two or three months.

But TAC refuses to take this. After Mlofana's murder, activists from the organization mobilized the community and campaigned for a trial that resulted in a life sentence for Mlofana's killers.

Twelve years ago, South Africa's new constitution guaranteed women full equality under the law, as part of the tumultuous transition from apartheid to democracy. But even though its Bill of Rights is one of the most extensive in the world, built on principles of human dignity, equality, and freedom, many women still face rampant rape and sexual violence.

At Simelela, a rape crisis center in Khayelitsha that partners with TAC, a woman's eyes look out hauntingly from a large black-and-white poster. "New South Africa?" asks the large, red-bordered letters. "Why are women still in the struggle?"

A Simelela pamphlet says that the rate of rape in Khayelitsha is one of the highest in the country. It also says that rates of reported rape throughout South Africa have gone up since the end of the apartheid regime.

But TAC counselor Ntlontlo says this does not mean there are more rapes happening than before. Instead, she says, it reflects the fact that more women are feeling empowered to report being raped.

Empowerment is something Ntlontlo knows about.

She was raped by a family member when she was only eight years old. "I lost my self-esteem," she says. "I lost my dignity."

After being raped, Ntlontlo initially told no one. As she grew older, she says she dealt with the trauma by having sex with multiple partners. Eventually she contracted HIV.

"People think HIV is the killer, but it is nothing compared to rape," Ntlontlo says in a Simelela profile. "Being raped is like being killed. When I found out I was HIV positive I just thought, if I survived rape I can survive anything."

Today, Ntlontlo is open about her status as a rape survivor living with HIV, and counsels other women to speak out about their experiences. "The more I talk about it, the more I feel stronger," she says.

Sharing this strength is something of a calling for Ntlontlo. Originally, she planned on being a lawyer to protect young girls who had been victimized. But when she could not afford to continue with law school, she became a counselor at TAC.

"I just told myself that I need to help others," Ntlontlo says. "I never got the help when I was raped."

Today, Simelela and TAC both run campaigns to educate children about HIV and as sexual abuse. Some of their outreach programs take place in primary schools.

Pumezi Rumeyi, who works at TAC, says the organization is often asked why they talk about HIV with young children.

"Where do we think they are going to get HIV?" says Runeyi. She points to rape and incest as causes of child HIV infection.

In 2000, HIV-related illnesses accounted for about one third of the deaths of those under five years old, according to South Africa's Medical Research Council.

In Langa, another Western Cape township, a group of preschool children recite a chant at their teachers' prompting: "My body. My body is special. I love my body. No one can touch my body. No one can abuse my body."

Ntutu, an organizer at Simelela, says her organization focuses on making children aware of what cannot be done to them—and "empowering them to tell" if they are abused.

Fifteen years after her rape, Ntlontlo made the decision to open a case. However, she was told there was not enough evidence. "Which evidence do they want?" asks Ntlontlo bitterly.

Recently, a family friend of former Vice President Jacob Zuma accused him of raping her. Zuma, who is now a leading candidate to replace Thabo Mbeki as president in 2009, testified that they had had consensual sex. He was eventually acquitted.

During the trial, the accuser was constantly harassed outside the courthouse by Zuma supporters. Taken into account during the testimony were her clothing and behavior.

Ntutu says that all too often women are blamed for being raped. She cites police and judges who claim that wearing a short skirt or going out at night is asking for trouble. One of the programs at Simelela focuses on training police to be sensitive to the needs of rape survivors.

The Zuma trial was further complicated by the fact that the accuser is HIV positive. Zuma said he thought he would be protected from the virus because he showered after sex.

This is characteristic of the misinformation coming from some higher-up government officials surrounding HIV/AIDS.

The Zuma case has had "quite a chilling effect" on women reporting rape, says Jody Kollapen, head of South Africa's Human Rights Commission.

Other obstacles in the justice system include "poor investigation, failure to arrest suspects, inadequate bail conditions, lengthy delays before trial, dockets going 'missing' and the harsh adversarial court environment," according to Simelela literature.

"We've been going to court and there's no progress," says Lungelo Yozi. Yozi, who works at TAC, says he got involved with the organization because both his mother and sister are HIV positive.

Kollapen believes that factors such as high unemployment, drugs and alcohol, and guns are part of what leads to the high incidence of violence against women. "A human becomes the object of this anger, this frustration," he says. "We know these things happen all the time."

Ntlontlo also says male unemployment is a factor in gender-based violence. "People are not working, they're sitting there doing nothing," she says. She says unemployed men become frustrated when women will not talk to them, and some of them become rapists.

In Khayelitsha, unemployment is as high as 80 percent, according to the South African Minister of Safety and Security. Kollapen says he believes unemployment is higher for men than for women.

However, he says he is "not suggesting poverty leads to crime, because that would be a supreme insult to those who are poor."

Simelela and TAC agree. "It is not poverty that leads people to rape, but community attitudes toward women and sexual violence, and it is these that must be changed," says Simelela in its literature.

According to the literature, men rape women to exert power, control, and ownership and because certain forms of rape are considered culturally acceptable.

The ABC system (abstain, be faithful, and condomise) is currently the leading method being taught to prevent HIV around the world. But a groundbreaking new type of HIV prevention, microbicides, is currently being developed.

Microbicides, which are not yet available, would be the only product other than condoms that protects against HIV. They would be applied topically in a form such as a gel, cream, or sponge.

Boniswa Seti says there was a conference about microbicides at TAC, where she works, in 2006. She says the new contraceptive "would help a great deal." Unlike condoms, microbicides do not require a partner's cooperation to use.

Microbicides could also benefit women who are already HIV positive, protecting them from re-infection, from other sexually transmitted infections, and from spreading HIV to their partners.

"It gives women—young women—power over their own choices," says Seti.

Fumana Ntlontlo, meanwhile, is doing her part to give young women power. Through her work at TAC, she says, "we are trying by all means to give the information that if you are raped you don't have to be quiet."

Ntlontlo says that although initially she felt her rapist had taken her dignity, she has realized that dignity is "like a tree; it grows back."

The one thing her rapist did not take from her was the tree's roots.

As women, "we need to be strong," says Ntlontlo. "Sometimes not for ourselves, but for others."

Drugs, rape and HIV—
South Africa's perfect storm

By Elena Larson
Khayelitsha, South Africa

"I lost the will to live," said the twenty-four-year-old rape survivor.

"All I wanted to do was die. I lost my job and even thought about taking drugs—anything to make the memories go away."

Her story, recorded at the Simelela Rape Crisis Center outside Cape Town, is not uncommon, according to Simelala counselors. They say it is often connected with drugs, especially *tik*, South Africa's version of what Americans call "ice" (crystal methamphetamine).

Easy to manufacture, tik is said to produce the same high and the same aggressive behavior as crack cocaine but, unlike crack, which lasts a relatively short time, a tik high can last up to four hours.

Already the country with the world's highest rape rate at 120 per 100,000 in 2006 (four times that of the United States) and the highest incidence of HIV/AIDS, as well as record rates of other violent crimes, South Africa is rapidly becoming home to a devastating drug addiction. Health workers say the phenomena are closely linked, and that any solution must take this into account.

Drug-related crimes in the Western Cape increased by 159 percent from 2001 to 2006, with a total of almost 35,000 reported that year, the most of any South African province, according to Safety and Security Minister Charles Nqakula.

Experts say the connection between drugs and aggressive behavior is strong. A 2002 study by the Institute for Security Studies (ISS), a regional research organization, found that more than 45 percent of those arrested for serious crimes over a two-year period tested positive for illegal substances.

"What this study does show is that drug use is common among people arrested for committing a wide range of crimes," says the ISS. "While we cannot say that most drug users are criminals, we can say that many criminals use drugs."

Nazma Hendriks, a counseling coordinator at the Rape Crisis Center in Manenburg where she has debriefed dozens of rape victims, told the South African daily *Die Burger* that there is "definitely a link" between tik and rape.

As a methamphetamine, tik triggers the release of chemicals like epinephrine and dopamine in the brain, which cause feelings like euphoria, increased confidence, and a heightened sense of sexuality, she said.

These feelings lead some to use tik as a date rape drug in order to increase libido. "Women who are about to be raped are forced to use it first. The rapists apparently believe that tik heightens the quality of the sexual experience. That is, of course, not true," Hendriks said.

In addition, tik is known to cause memory loss, which puts survivors at a disadvantage in court because their testimonies are not considered trustworthy. "Rape survivors can't always remember what happened, and, therefore, aren't reliable witnesses in court," she said.

Tik's association with increased libido also puts survivor's testimonies at a disadvantage, as their resistance to the act is more likely to be questioned, according to Hendricks.

In this way, the legal process becomes increasingly difficult for rape survivors when tik is involved. "I wanted to press charges. I wanted him to go to prison. Until I knew he was behind bars I wouldn't feel safe. But it is not an easy process and sometimes I feel like giving up," one twenty-seven-year-old rape survivor told Simelela.

HIV transmission is a common result of rape whose likelihood increases with the use of tik, according to the Cape Town Women's Health Co-Op. Its literature cites a study that shows that tik users are less likely to have safe sex, as they have higher numbers of sexual partners and more unprotected sex than non-tik users.

In addition, tik can be dehydrating, drying out the skin and causing tears in the vagina, anus, and mouth. In doing so, it makes the transmission of HIV and other sexually transmitted infections much more likely.

Commonly sold in cold drink straws, pinched tight at each end, tik is often smoked in lightbulbs heated from below after their metal screw bases are removed. One straw typically sells for

R15 to R30 ($2 to $4) and can be made from local ingredients, such as battery acid, antifreeze, lye, or over-the-counter cold medications containing ephedrine, according to the Cape Town Drug Counseling Centre (CTDCC).

Local drug counselors say that anyone with a high-school knowledge of chemistry can manufacture it, because the recipe is accessible over the Internet.

The rapid rise in tik's use since 2002 worries Cape Town researchers. "Nowhere else in the world has there been such a massive increase in the use of a drug over such a short period of time," CTDCC director Grant Jardine told the *Mail & Guardian*, adding that "most users are involved in crime or prostitution to fund their habit."

Andreas Plüddermann, a senior researcher at the Medical Research Council, has called for stepped up efforts to understand these connections: "There is an urgent need for research, not only to assess the prevalence of tik, but also to get a better understanding of the link between tik use and mental health problems and sexual risk behavior."

Meanwhile, MDC officials have taken to calling Cape Town "the tik capital of South Africa."

TAC takes on HIV/AIDS

By Erika Fields
Cape Town, South Africa

Brightly colored posters on the faintly painted walls provide information to anyone entering the room. The messages vary from warnings of violence against women to information about sexual transmitted infections and HIV/AIDS.

Inside, three young activists sit with their backs to the wall, ready to provide more information to those waiting for help.

Each has personal reasons for being here, like the young woman who had a cousin affected by the disease, but they are all working together to solve the same problem: HIV/AIDS in South Africa.

These two women and one man are part of a small group of twenty-three individuals who work with the Treatment Action Campaign (TAC) of Khayelitsha, a township of more than 350,000 persons on the outskirts of Cape Town.

In Khayelitsha, there are an estimated 40,000 people living with HIV/AIDS. But throughout the country, an estimated 5.5 million people are infected.

TAC began its program in 1998 to pressure the South African government into fighting the battle with HIV/AIDS.

"We campaign for treatment for people with HIV and to reduce new HIV infections. Our efforts have resulted in many life-saving interventions, including the implementation of country-wide mother-to-child transmission prevention and antiretroviral treatment programmes," says the TAC Web site.

"A big challenge in TAC's early years was our own leadership's lack of knowledge about HIV," says an unsigned article in the organization's monthly magazine *Equal Treatment.*

But since then, TAC says it has gone into poor communities, like Khayelitsha, to educate the people there.

"HIV education has given people with HIV dignity and the knowledge to take control of their lives," according to "Equal

Treatment." "It is arguably the most important work that TAC does." TAC also campaigns for access to affordable treatment, supports the prevention and elimination of HIV/AIDS, and challenges legislation through lobbying, advocacy and litagation.

TAC claims that its treatment literacy program has worked and is saving lives in communities throughout the Cape region.

By the end of 2005, there were 5.5 million people living with HIV in South Africa, with almost 1,000 AIDS deaths occurring every day, according to Avert, a major international HIV/AIDS organization.

In 2005, more than 700 people were diagnosed with HIV per month, with an average of 327 new patients enrolled in HIV clinics, though approximately 45 percent of the newly diagnosed did not come to the clinics to follow up with HIV services, according to the 2006 Annual Activity Report in Khayelitsha.

"The total number of consultations in the three dedicated HIV clinics in Khayelitsha continued to increase sharply in 2005 with a total of 56,547 consultations compared to 40,019 in the previous year, a 41 percent increase," according to the Annual Activity Report.

TAC publications say the organization has educated 600 police from the South African Crime Protection unit in Gauteng. Of those that attended, about half went for voluntary counseling and testing after the training. Not only were the police informed about HIV/AIDS, they are now able to direct individuals to this program.

Also, in the province of Limpopo, doctors had been distributing the wrong treatment regimens. But after TAC's treatment literacy practitioners intervened, this stopped happening.

Organizations like TAC are not the only ones fighting HIV/AIDS.

In another part of Khayelitsha, Silvia Khuselo runs a soup kitchen out of her home on Mondays to provide food for HIV-positive people. Although she receives little to no help from any organization, she says she continues to help people who have no one else.

Most of the money comes from personal charities, says Khuselo. But she now receives a small amount of money from HOPE Worldwide, an organization that provides money for HIV-positive adults.

Critics say the South African government is not doing enough to help people that have HIV/AIDS and to prevent the further spread of the disease.

"The South African government was initially hesitant about providing antiretroviral treatment to HIV-positive people, and only started to supply the drugs in 2004 – years after many other nations had begun to do so – following pressure from activists," says Avert. "Even since 2004, the distribution of has been relatively slow, with only around 33 percent of people in need receiving treatment at the end of 2006."

South Africa is in a crisis, but nothing is being done, says activist Bernadette Ross, who works for an organization that helps children and adults affected by HIV/AIDS. She wants the government to do more to help them, instead of just relying on organizations like hers.

An estimated 5.5 million out of an estimated population of 47 million are living with HIV/AIDS in South Africa, according to a 2006 Report on the Global AIDS Epidemic. The report says an estimated 320,000 deaths were related to AIDS. Only 21 percent of those affected with HIV/AIDS received antiretroviral drugs (ARVs).

TAC members are trying to stretch themselves to help everyone they can, but that is not enough, says TAC activist Lungelo Yuzi.

Despite the criticism, government officials maintain they have made an effort to move forward in the fight against HIV/AIDS.

Health Minister Manto Tshabalala-Msimang said that more than $27 million of her budget would be spent during the next two years on warning South Africans about the virus, according to *The Cape Times*.

She claims that in the last financial year, more than 400 million male condoms and more than 3 million female condoms were distributed to the people. She also says that 439,000 patients with debilitating conditions received nutritional support from the government and 282,236 patients have been treated with antiretroviral drugs.

Recently, a plan was submitted to the South African National AIDS Council that will become the new national AIDS policy, binding not only the government of South Africa, but all those who have been involved with developing and refining the plan, according to *Equal Treatment*.

"This [policy] describes the implications of the Constitutional right to health. It describes what it will mean to create a social environment which respects the rights of people with, affected by and vulnerable to HIV infection," says the TAC newsletter.

The new plan sets out the government's commitment to respond to the HIV/AIDS epidemic in South Africa until 2011. "It recognizes the critical duty of leadership from government, but assigns responsibility to every sector of society for its implication. It is a source of hope for people with HIV and their families," says the TAC newsletter. "If implemented properly, it will save millions of lives."

For its part, the United States Consulate claims that its number one priority in South Africa is the fight against HIV/AIDS.

"I think it's important that we succeed here," says Consul General Helen La Lime.

With help from the U.S., 500,000 South Africans will receive ARVs. But the jury is still out on whether the program is working, says La Lime.

In 2004, the U.S. program received $90 million, while this year, the program received $370 million, says La Lime, who expects that next year's program will be almost $600 million.

She says that the U.S. Government wants to raise the amount of money used to fight the HIV/AIDS battle to $30 billion over the next five years.

The U.S. is caring for orphans and helping with ARVs, but it is not clear if they are making enough progress to curb the spread of the disease, and that is key, says La Lime.

If South Africa, with all its resources, fails in the battle against HIV/AIDS, she asks, what are the prospects likely to be for the rest of the continent?

South Africans push government on HIV/AIDS

By Beth Maclin
Cape Town, South Africa

Sitting at the end of the coffee shop counter, a cell phone glued to his ear, twenty-three-year-old Julian Simcock gives an arriving stranger an inquisitive glance. After realizing this is the person he is waiting for, he says goodbye and puts away his phone. He folds up his newspaper and pushes his empty coffee cup and saucer to the side, clearing space on the wooden counter.

Simcock speaks with a slight accent, indicative of his youth in New Zealand and most likely brought back from spending the last year-and-a-half in another former British colony as a Fulbright scholar, but with his fading tan, precisely-styled "casual" hair, and button-down blue cotton shirt, he looks like a typical American graduate student—which he is.

On first appearances alone, he seems an unlikely coworker and confidante of someone the *New Yorker* once called the "AIDS Rebel," Zackie Achmat, co-founder and chairperson of the Treatment Action Campaign (TAC). But as he tells his story, it rapidly becomes obvious that he is that and much more.

Simcock says he did not come to South Africa with the intent to learn about HIV/AIDS, and definitely did not think he would end up working closely with Achmat on a range of projects relating to the high costs of the epidemic on society. But, he adds, the time he spent as a researcher for TAC was "hugely informative."

"I came holding some of the same reticence about HIV/AIDS that most people have, and meeting Zachie and working so closely with somebody everyday who has HIV is a very sort of personal and real way of countering those stigmatizations," says Simcock.

"You meet somebody and spend time with somebody who works around the clock like Zachie does, and is on top of it, and as charismatic as Zachie is, it reduces even any lingering thoughts about whether HIV is as debilitating as people say it is."

Three leading research groups found that between 4.5 and 5.7

million South Africans were HIV positive in the middle of 2006, according to the University of Pretoria's Centre for the Study of AIDS (CSA). With a population of 48 million, this gives South Africa one of the highest HIV infection rates in the world.

Yet the post-apartheid government of President Thabo Mbeki has been slow to respond to this problem, and independent organizations have had to fill the gap.

TAC is one of these organizations.

With its more than sixty employees and 16,000 volunteers, however, TAC only has one worker for every 330 South Africans with HIV that needs help.

"I wouldn't want this to end up in a South African newspaper, but the people of the Treatment Action Campaign are tired," says Simcock. "It's like fighting a long war."

TAC fills a gap

TAC was started in 1998 out of a need for nevirapine, a drug that prevents mother-to-child transmission of HIV but that the government was not supplying, according to Simcock.

"Many health care professionals had become frustrated by the government's lack of progress in supplying the drug, which, the government argued, was due to questions about its toxicity. Doctors had started applying to non-governmental organizations for grants to pay for nevirapine, and in some cases used their own money to buy the drug," according to the British charity AVERT. Doctors who provided the drug risked termination because doing so was forbidden.

"[TAC] was intended, to begin with, to challenge pharmaceutical companies at a time when pharmaceutical companies were able to charge huge rates. I think for a while in the states it cost $10,000 a year to treat someone with anti-retroviral medication. But obviously prices have come down since then, but it's been an ongoing battle for generic medication," says Simcock.

He speaks highly of Achmat and sits up a little straighter and speaks a bit faster when talking about one of the most highly publicized instances of AIDS activism here—when Achmat went to Thailand and attempted to bring back econazol, a generic-priced drug, to South Africa, which is illegal.

"The numbers are easy to calculate—how many more people could be treated? And that was a powerful thing. It openly defied a law, and Zackie was never trying to hide that. But for the purpose of the public, to one, to challenge whether the law is just, and two, to bring people's attention to the very real discrepancies that exist," he says.

Another TAC action that got a lot of media attention came in March 2003, when the organization charged the Health Minister and her Trade and Industry colleague with culpable homicide.

During a speech soon after charges were pressed, a TAC representative told Health Minister Mantombazana Edmie Tshabalala-Msimang: "We are angry. According to government's sources over 600 people will die of AIDS every day on average this year. We stand here today to say to you that you have willfully and negligently failed to implement the necessary interventions, including antiretroviral treatment, that would prevent many of these deaths."

TAC has used the courts in South Africa both to ally with the government against pharmaceutical companies and to challenge the government over its own practices. "They didn't perceive at the outset that it was going to be this long a fight with the government," says Simcock.

TAC also focuses on the issues of education, particularly breaking down the stereotypes of HIV/AIDS.

A large problem with the fight against HIV/AIDS is making people aware of "the scientific and medical reality of HIV/AIDS, which has become a hugely important task since the government, as you must know, champion a different set of policies somtimes," says Simcock.

Because of widespread public ignorance on the issue, there is also a stigma attached to people with the virus that causes AIDS. One tactic TAC has used to change this is to distribute T-shirts that say "HIV Positive." The idea came from the actions of the Danish king when the Nazis were set to invade, says Simcock.

When the Nazis told him to have all Jews in Denmark wear a yellow star, making it easy for them to be found, the king encouraged all Danes to wear the star and did so himself. This helped the Jews feel accepted in the community and made it difficult for the Nazis to find their targets. Simcock says the TAC T-shirts follow the same logic.

"The HIV Positive T-shirts aren't limited to people who have HIV," says Simcock. "The idea is actually opposite—that you can't tell who has HIV just by looking at them and that there shouldn't be a stigma."

The third part of TAC's work, after lobbying and education, is service delivery. An example of this can be seen in the clinic set up in Sight B of Khayelitsha, the largest township outside of Cape Town. The clinic was opened in 2001 and is a partnership between the Western Cape Health Department and MSF.

"The idea isn't to one day assume the HIV/AIDS service delivery responsibility for South Africa," says Simcock. "It's to sort of push the government where they need pushing to provide more comprehensive coverage.

"And the way to do that, in some instances, is to prove to the government and to the world that you can be in a place where there's very limited resources, where there's often very little education and low rates of literacy and those sorts of things, you can change HIV/AIDS. You can change the epidemic."

HIV/AIDS in South Africa

Between 1993 and 2000, South Africa experienced a huge increase in the instances of HIV/AIDS when the country was focused on the transition between the apartheid regime and the newly-elected democratic government. The economic emphasis on mining, which required men to live in single-sex housing for extended periods of time, and the government's unwillingness to address the problem made South Africa extremely vulnerable.

"It's sort of the unfortunate issue that if the government had been more cognizant early on, been more honest early on, a huge amount of damage could have been prevented and now it's grown to the point of mammoth proportions," says Simcock. "Now it's very difficult to do without a huge investment."

The executive director of UNAIDS, Dr. Peter Piot, said in a presentation earlier this year that the prevalence of AIDS in southern Africa is because of "decades of colonialism, migration, gender inequality and apartheid, combined with denial and inadequate action on AIDS."

The accepted medical field treatment for HIV is taking antiretrovirals (ARV), something the government has been slow to provide and pharmaceutical companies have made more difficult by maintaining high prices.

"Amongst the scientific community there is little doubt about the benefits of ARVs; a recent study in South Africa reported that

93% of HIV positive people surveyed were alive after one year of treatment," according to the Integrated Regional Information Network, the UN's humanitarian news and analysis service in Africa.

In South Africa, because the dispersal of ARVs is limited, Piot says three people become infected with HIV for every one person who starts ARV therapy. "If we don't reduce infection levels today, tomorrow's treatment bills will be exorbitant. And millions more will die," he says.

The CSA report projects that introducing a comprehensive ARV program now, delayed as it is, would have a dramatic impact on the number of AIDS deaths per year.

Without ARVs, it is expected that South Africa will experience 505,000 deaths a year by 2010. However, with ARVs, the projected number of deaths drops by more than 100,000 to 388,000 a year. Furthermore, the CSA report suggests that if 90 percent of people with HIV were to receive treatment, the number could drop further to 291,000.

The possible impact of ARVs on the number of deaths a year is heavily contingent on the service delivery by the government, which does not have a strong track record, but has shown progress in recent months under different leadership.

The Mbeki government started supplying the drugs in 2004, but has been slow to reach all who need it. "Even since 2004, the distribution of antiretroviral drugs has been relatively slow, with only around 33% of people in need receiving treatment at the end of 2006," according to the World Health Organization Web site.

The CSA report estimates that in 2006, 225,000 of the 711,000 people needing ARVs received it. Because of the rapid increase in new cases of HIV, by 2015, even if coverage dropped to 20 percent, 500,000 people would be receiving it and if it increased to 90 percent, two million people would be on it.

One obstacle in the way of rolling out ARVs is price. "The government had frequently argued that an increase in access to antiretroviral treatment was not necessarily the best way to stop the AIDS epidemic, and that other treatment options needed to be considered," says AVERT in a Web-based critique.

Those pushing for access to cheaper prices for the medication achieved a victory in a court case when several pharmaceutical companies, including GlaxoSmithKline, agreed to allow low-cost versions of their drugs to be made in South Africa, according to the BBC.

Another cost, often not part of the debate over providing treatment to those living with HIV, is the ripple-effect impact on society.

"What I've learned since is the way that HIV/AIDS is connected to so many things—social forces, political forces, and economics forces," says Simcock. "And so, with the numbers that are this high and people are dying at this rate, it has profound consequences well beyond the health sector or well beyond mortality rates.

"I mean, you have in some age groups, one in five teachers affected with the disease. And you can't afford to have one in five teachers, and you can't afford to have your nurses sick because you need the nurses there to treat AIDS-related illnesses and other illnesses. And then you get into the realm of children who have been orphaned by AIDS."

Simcock believes that there is money available for these drugs, and it is an issue of the government prioritizing what it wants to spend it on: "I mean keeping people alive, if that isn't one of your priorities, then I struggle to know how prioritization is working. But, there is money. There is definitely money. The government is running a surplus at the moment.

"There have been a lot of ministries that don't spend their allocations. It's about capacity. They need a huge increase in nurses and professionals in the health care industry. And they need to enlist, in some cases, the private sector. And they're dragging their feet because of politics and because of not wanting to increase jobs, but there's no time for it as far as people who have the disease are concerned."

AIDS "denialism" starts at the top

Some officials in the South African government, including President Thabo Mbeki and Health Minister Tshabalala-Msimang, are under fire for their questioning of the link between HIV and AIDS, as well as the best way to treat HIV.

"The biggest problem we have in South Africa is that we have a president who doesn't believe that HIV causes AIDS," Achmat told the *Mail & Guardian*, one of South Africa's leading newspapers.

Desmond Tutu, winner of the Nobel Peace Prize and a former Anglican archbishop, is also critical of the current administration, especially Tshabalala-Msimang's suggestion that nutrition is as important as ARVs in treating HIV.

"We are playing with the lives of people, with the lives of mothers who would not have died if they had had drugs. If people want garlic and potatoes let them have them, but let's not play games. Stop all this discussion about garlic," he told IRIN.

"South Africa is the unkindest cut of all," said Stephen Lewis, UN Special Envoy for HIV/AIDS in Africa, at the 2006 Inter-national AIDS Conference in Toronto. Lewis called it the only country in Africa "whose government is still obtuse, dilatory and negligent about rolling out treatment."

"It is the only country in Africa whose government continues to propound theories more worthy of a lunatic fringe than of a concerned and compassionate state," he added. "I'm of the opinion that they can never achieve redemption."

The South African government received a letter titled "Expression of Concern by HIV Scientists" late last year from more than eighty scientists, including the co-discoverer of AIDS, Robert Gallo, calling for the immediate removal of Dr. Tshabalala-Msimang as Minister of Health.

The letter also called for "an end to the disastrous, pseudo-scientific policies that have characterised the South African Government's response to HIV/AIDS."

Simcock says that the lack of strong leadership is the biggest disadvantage South Africa has in the fight against HIV/AIDS. He cites the successes of Brazil and Thailand and acknowledges that they were based on leadership.

"Members of the South African government have constantly reiterated that ARVs are just one aspect of their treatment approach, and that there are other measures that can help to treat HIV. Manto Tshabalala-Msimang has questioned the effectiveness of ARVs, and famously urges people to eat lots of beetroot and garlic to fight off HIV," says AVERT.

"At the 2006 International AIDS Conference in Toronto, these food products were even displayed prominently on South Africa's exhibition stand. Allegedly, ARVs were only added to the display when reporters started to question their absence."

The health minister has also supported the Dr. Rath Health Foundation, an organization that pushes vitamin supplements instead of ARVs. "The foundation has previously published adverts in South Africa claiming that ARVs are toxic and cause AIDS," says AVERT. "The TAC has strongly criticised the government for failing to condemn the organization."

The former South African deputy president, Jacob Zuma—a leading candidate to replace Mbeki in the 2009 presidential elections—also caused controversy over how to properly treat HIV in 2006 when he claimed that taking a shower after having sex with a HIV-positive woman would prevent him from contracting it, according to the BBC.

Simcock believes that spreading this information makes them responsible for deaths: "That has cost lives. I mean at a very fundamental level, those people are responsible for deaths, right? Because they're spreading incorrect information and they know better, there's plenty of access to the truth.

"They're spreading incorrect information in that, if you're a fourteen or fifteen-year-old teenager in South Africa, and you listen to what your health minister has to tell you, which should be a trusted figure of authority, you're not going to think very hard about the dangers of HIV and AIDS, and where's the incentive then to use a condom?"

Simcock says that he and many South Africans are unsure of the reasons behind the government's response to the epidemic. He likened it to the debate among Americans over why the Bush administration went to war with Iraq.

"I mean on the surface, because someone thought this guy was dangerous and had weapons of mass destruction. Underneath that, who knows? If they knew he didn't have those things, it must have been some other reason," he says.

"So that plagues the conversation in South Africa, too. One, which is not speculated, it's true, is that there was an encouragement for one reason or another of this pseudo-science, these denialists and pseudo-scientists were flown in from all over the world to speak with the president and give this appearance of credibility of criticizing antiretrovirals."

"So that's definitely part of it, that there was some belief, at least for a little while, condemning antiretrovirals and suggesting in some cases HIV doesn't cause AIDS or AIDS doesn't exist," says Simcock. "It's just malaria that kills people. It's just tuberculosis that kills people. And all those things are not helped by the complexity of AIDS.

"I mean the reason AIDS is called AIDS, acquired immunodeficiency syndrome, the reason it's called syndrome, is because it's a series of symptoms. You don't have one disease. You have something that is killing your immune system and exposes it to other diseases that are eventually what kills you. So, that lends itself to mischievous stuff.

"One of the other reasons is the suggestion, I think, that there isn't the money to pay for the drugs, and that's accompanied by all sorts of things, like if we give people antiretrovirals they'll just live longer and keep spreading the disease and that will kill more people," says Simcock. "And one of the good things about that is that antiretrovirals actually reduce your infectiousness."

Simcock acknowledges that not all members of the government are in this highly-criticized group, and that some have been very helpful.

"There's huge, huge progress over the past couple of months and that's been, for me, wonderful and a historic thing to watch. History in South Africa really does unfold on a daily basis," says Simcock. "Here, the Deputy Minister of Health, Nozizwe Madlala-Routledge, she's been an incredible leader in the health department.

"And the Deputy President, as well, has been a leadership figure. That's not to say that there aren't still plenty of denialists. Manto Tshabalala-Msimang was reinstated as the Health Minister," he says.

"People believe government authorities," says Simcock. "Those government authorities have an obligation to use truth and it sounds like a trite thing to say, and a simplistic thing to say, and they do, a moral and professional obligation."

Women balance home and family to pursue their passion for art at Funda Community College, Soweto. (Dan Connell/The Image Works)

A people's mural greets visitors to the Funda Community College in Soweto. (Erika Fields)

Funda art school director Charles Nkosi introduces visitors to the college's sculpture garden. (Dan Connell/The Image Works)

Women artists share their stories and display their work at the
Funda Community College. (Dan Connell/The Image Works)

Artist Paula Mazibuko describes her work to visiting Simmons
reporters. (Dan Connell/The Image Works)

Nongovernmental organizations run family planning clinics in poor communities not served by government facilities. (Dan Connell/The Image Works)

HIV/AIDS is a central focus for counselors at the Simelela Rape Crisis Center in Khayelitsha. (Dan Connell/The Image Works)

Johannesburg's Apartheid Museum helps visitors experience apartheid while learning its history. (Dan Connell/The Image Works)

Simmons reporters take a day off to enjoy the nature reserve at Cape Point. (Dan Connell/The Image Works)

Visiting reporters are escorted through Khayelitsha by a group of aspiring young tour guides. (Dan Connell/The Image Works)

A stroll through the back streets of Khayelitsha reveals a vibrant community. (Dan Connell/The Image Works)

Reporter Kristin Pitts takes a moment to relax in Khayelitsha with her four "personal hairdressers." (Christina Lenis)

Student reporter Faythe Mallinger takes a break to play with her hosts. (Dan Connell/The Image Works)

Reporter Ashley Price compares the experiences of black South Africans and African Americans. (Dan Connell/The Image Works)

Cultural
Rights

Art as personal struggle

By Kristin Pitts
Soweto, South Africa

On the nights when Flora More is not feeling sad, she falls asleep with glue on her fingers, waiting for inspiration to hit.

When it does, More goes to her workspace, a six-by-four-foot corner of her parents' dimly-lit home. There she pushes aside small medicine bottles and tears into her limited stock of unconventional supplies, mostly scavenged from her neighbors' garbage, and, occasionally, if the shade of blue is just right, into a magazine, which she buys for a few rand.

The result invariably showcases More's now well-known trademarks: bright colors and South African women. But as her collages make their way off her thin partitions and onto the walls of posh hotels, homes and art galleries, the only thing that keeps up with the popularity of her women-focused work is the criticism of it.

The backlash, she says, stems from a powerful legacy of sexism and a deeply entrenched resistance to letting it go. Despite the fact that South Africa's new constitution protects women's rights and promotes equal opportunities, women find themselves in a constant battle for employment—and for respect.

More is one of them, but she refuses to be intimidated.

"Women here are being discriminated against by men," More says. "They think we only belong in the home, but we are trying to prove them wrong. Nothing is impossible, as long as you have a mind and the hands to do it."

In this post-apartheid society, where not long ago inequality was not just socially but legally enforced, More is looking for the balance in her own life and work that oppressed South Africans fought so long for in the political sphere.

"Men say all the time, 'Why are you only drawing women?'" More says. And, she adds, they are often put off by her "loathing."

The anger that infuses much of her work stems from her

experience as a woman living in Soweto, South Africa's largest black township—an experience she insists is typical.

A high school dropout, More married young to a man who abused her. When he died a few years later, she says, her community turned on her, accusing her of involvement in his death.

But it would not be long before her community would reject her a second time. A few years ago, More discovered that she, like tens of thousands of South African women, was HIV positive. After disclosing her status to her employer, she says she fell victim to both her disease and the ignorance surrounding it.

"Due to discriminations that I faced after I disclosed my status, I was sent away by my employer," More says. "Apparently they thought I was going to infect them."

In a country where as much misinformation on HIV is being spread as fact, stories like More's are all too common. South African Health Minister Tshabalala-Msimang's assertion that a diet of beetroot and garlic is vital in treating HIV, coupled with former Deputy President Jacob Zuma's claim that a shower after having sex could prevent HIV from being transmitted, are two recent examples of how the public has been misled at the highest levels on the nature of the disease and how to combat it.

But More considers herself lucky.

"I was fortunate to get a big project doing mosaic work, which sustained me for about a year, " she says. After her project was completed, More entered the workforce with a positive attitude, and with support from the few people who were willing to give it: her professors and classmates at Funda Community College.

"When I first started school, there was no one supporting me. But I stayed here, I persisted," More says looking around the room at other women artists, their work on display on the walls behind them. "I invited my friends and family to my first art exhibition, and that got me a little respect, and a little more when they did a story about me in the paper, but still people were asking 'Why are you doing this?'

"Finally I brought my work back home and hung it on the walls. That's when people fell in love with it."

More's work offers hope in a place where it is often hard to come by, where basic needs like housing, water and electricity are unaffordable commodities for many and where ostentatious wealth is just a taxi ride away.

For More and the five family members who lean on her for financial support, money for the basics is, for now, in place. But just how long that money will be there is the question that has been keeping More up late, blocking the anything-but-sad mood she says she relies on to work.

As an independent artist, More knows her next paycheck is not guaranteed. As an HIV-positive artist, that uncertainty is even more real.

Currently, More's CD4 count, which indicates the strength of her immune system, is under 200. Healthy, HIV-negative adults generally have a CD4 count of 500-1,500 cells per cubic millimeter of blood. Preventative treatment and government funding starts when a patient's CD4 count is under 200.

Once an HIV positive patient's CD4 count rises above 200, the patient is deemed well enough to go off government aid—a cut off that terrifies More as she reviews her already-tight budget.

That aid, along with the money she earns from her collages, goes to feed, clothe and house her son, a niece, a sister who works part time, and her parents, who receive a small pension. By the time her expenses are paid, she does not have much left over. But she has seen how bad it can get, she says, and considers herself fortunate.

A few months from now, More will take a CD4 test to determine whether or not she will continue receiving aide. She says she now finds herself in an internal tug-of-war: hoping for better health, but also hoping for a budget that supports her family.

More says she worries that getting better will mean that she will not be able to afford "luxury" items like electricity, or her son's education.

But she is not alone. With unemployment rates skyrocketing, "getting better" has become a relative term.

"I worry a lot," More says, "but after HIV, you have to be strong."

More stares into the distance for a while, then snaps back into the moment. Her worries have been getting to her—affecting her work. Sometimes she says she will find herself up at all hours of the night, adding or taking away from her latest collage, ignoring her commitment to only work when she is happy.

"Sometimes I work without thinking, and I have to stop, but it's hard. When you start tearing and creating it all feels right,"

More says. It is difficult to stop her glue-covered fingers when for so long collages have acted as a kind of therapy for her.

"You know what helps? This," she says, pointing out a collage of four women—her closest friends, who got her through her husband's death, her education and now HIV. "This helps. This and my son."

More leans back in her folding chair. She says she is tired but does not look it. Her eyes are wide and her skin is radiant. She seems to have found herself, in her successes and her struggles.

"This has changed me in so many ways. My thinking is more matured, and the way people think of me is different," More says, smiling. "They see a person now instead of just a lady."

Art as Politics

By Faythe Mallinger
Soweto, South Africa

Sun pours in through the deteriorated window, illuminating the paint-splattered linoleum floor. Colorful artwork decorates the pale yellow walls. In one corner hangs a striking image of two children sitting on the ground—one black, one white—made from multicolored scraps of cloth and paper.

The collage was created by a student in the Fine Arts Department of Funda Community College, whose other divisions include degree candidates—called matrics—as well as music and information technology. All four nestle together within South Africa's largest black township, Soweto, just outside Johannesburg, the country's financial hub.

In contrast with the drab structures of the other schools, the outer walls of the Fine Arts Department are decorated with color-ful murals depicting township life. One that shows a man pushing a wheelbarrow full of bricks and a woman with a baby welcomes visitors to the Funda Art Gallery. Even the simple brick patio is teeming with imaginative bronze animal sculptures.

But much of the student artwork depicts the country's transformation to democracy, including the cruelty that black South Africans endured under the racist apartheid system, which affected everyone—even artists.

Funda was founded in 1984 as challenges to apartheid were intensifying across the country, according to Fine Arts director Charles Nkosi, who says that school officials and students were forced to deal with state-imposed restrictions to artistic expression, including the censorship of all political material that was critical of the apartheid government.

One year after Funda's establishment, the government declared a state of emergency in the Eastern Cape and the Pretoria-Witwatersrand-Vereeniging regions. This was extended to the entire country by 1986.

The emergency—under which nearly all civil rights were suspended—was a response to growing civil unrest in South Africa's black and "colored" townships, where the banned African National Congress—now the ruling party—was waging a campaign to make the communities "ungovernable." Security forces were sent to Soweto and other townships to control the country's protesting black residents.

As many as 24,000 people, mainly young black men, were detained without trial as soldiers replaced police in the townships, according to a human rights report from that period.

Threats of punishment for speaking out against the government had a large impact on the information that was being distributed to the people, with newspapers shut down and reporters prohibited from witnessing, let alone writing about, anti-apartheid protests. Meanwhile, the government controlled all TV and radio.

Nor were other forms of expression immune to censorship. "The Minister of the Interior passed legislation to ban publications found to be 'undesirable' for reasons such as 'obscenity, moral harmfulness, blasphemy, and causing harm,'" says Ahmed Motala, the director of the Human Rights Institute of South Africa.

Funda's Nkosi remembers the impact that the state of emergency had on art throughout the 1980s. He says he joined the school's faculty in 1986 at the height of governmental restrictions on expression.

"All the black artists were reflecting things that were happening around them," says Nkosi, adding that common themes included trade union organizing and the campaign to release Nelson Mandela from prison. Others focused on specific issues and incidents, such as the hated pass laws, police shootings and detentions that were an integral part of township life during the apartheid era.

But these visual forms of protest and resistance did not go unpunished.

Nkosi says he remembers fellow artists being questioned about the content of their work. Following his participation in the 1982 Botswana Festival of Culture and Resistance, he, too, became the object of interrogation. The event was largely dominated by followers of the "Black Consciousness" movement, which advocated solidarity among black South Africans and black leadership in the liberation struggle. Agents of the Special Branch—South Africa's apartheid-era secret police—paid Nkosi a visit upon his return from the festival.

Anyone found working on anything controversial had to suffer the consequences, he says.

But censorship did not stop at mere questioning. Some artists had their work vandalized or completely destroyed by apartheid supporters.

"In 1991 one of my sculptures entitled 'Eugene Terre'Blanche and his Two Sidekicks' (1989), in the collection of the South African Art Gallery, was destroyed in the gallery by six members of the Afrikaner Weerstandsbeweging, the AWB. Some protest art elicited strong, even extreme, reactions of censorship or physical destruction," South African artist Gael Neke told a 1999 Truth and Reconciliation Commission conference.

"The censorship affected every aspect of cultural, intellectual and educational life, and although grimly menacing, the magnitude of the banning of ANC-symbols; buttons, T-shirts and lighters included, was truly paranoid," says author and artist Mette Newth, a founder of the Norwegian Forum for Freedom of Expression.

After South Africa's first democratic election in 1994 and the adoption of a new constitution two years later that guaranteed the right of free expression to all the country's citizens—and "freedom of artistic creativity"—artists finally had the chance to ply their trade without strict boundaries. And at Funda that is just what they are doing.

"[Art is] the blessing of being able to share your experiences with other people," Nkosi says, smiling.

Art as activism

Sheenan Ashley Price
Johannesburg, South Africa

"Which pair should I get? I just can't decide," I ask.

"Get both pair," she says.

We both laugh. I consider it but realize I don't have enough rand with me.

The green and blue pair are practical. But there is just something about that yellow and blue that keeps catching my eye.

I pick the pair I like. I pay. I feel satisfied and amazed.

The jewelry on display here ranges from bright oranges, intense greens and blues, splashes of yellow, pretty purples and candy apple reds.

They are all made of recycled soda cans.

The Sprite can finally appeals to me the most. Even though the orange and purple Fantas scream, "Take me, take me," I give in to my childhood obsession with Sprite and take the green and blue earrings rolled with thin silver wire around the center.

But nothing tops the necklace made from a Coca-Cola can. It is simply a sight to see, and the purchase touches me deeply.

I am supporting not only the art but a women's organization whose focus is finding healing through art. I am also supporting a black woman who has decided to be a full-time artist—a simple declaration to some but a major decision for a black woman in a country only thirteen years free of apartheid's repressive rule.

Bongi Mkhize is a former student at Funda Community College. She has come back for the day to meet with a visiting student group.

Funda was established in 1984 as an alternative for students who left school after the 1976 student uprising in this restive black township, South Africa's largest. Now a school of great caliber, the Fine Arts Department houses students from the Eastern and Western Cape and as far away as Angola and Swaziland.

Mkhize is one of hundreds who have taken part in this revolutionary department. She studied here for three years after entering with an interest in fashion design, but she fell in love with visual art and has since dedicated her life to creating "reflective art."

When she is not in her studio creating her own pieces, Mkhize is in schools teaching small children. She focuses on print-making around HIV/AIDS with her students and has them - interpret their understanding of the disease through their art. "This helps them to better understand. It makes it real," she says.

Mkhize also works with a women's organization called the Siyavaya Arts Explosion, whose goal is to help women who come from abusive situations to deal and heal through art. The women create art from recycled items, and Mkhize helps them sell their creations. She speaks of her work with the organization with much enthusiasm. "I am working to get a Web site up," she says.

She thanks me for my purchase and quickly packs the jewelry away. "I'm on my way to another meeting, and I hope to sell more jewelry there," she says as she makes her way to the door.

Reflections

At home in their home

By Faythe Mallinger
Khayelitsha, South Africa

This is her home.

I remind myself of this several times over the course of our twelve-hour stay in the tiny two-bedroom bungalow.

Here is the bucket, says Vicky, the owner of a nearby B&B and our host in the township, pointing at the green plastic pail before she double-locks the door and leaves us alone in our overnight accommodation.

The two guest rooms of Vicky's bed and breakfast cannot board all twelve in our group, so she has outsourced some of us to a friend and guided us through a warren of narrow paths and darkened back streets to get there.

We cannot use the outhouse at night—it is not safe, says the owner of the residence, who also leaves to stay at another neighbor's house. Our student group is here to document the status of human rights in post-apartheid South Africa, but we are getting a large dose of South African hospitality at the same time.

I have never used a bucket for anything more than building sandcastles at the beach. My own house has three toilets—three toilets for four people.

Two of us will share a double bed that is adorned with a hand-made white-and-red satin comforter. Flowers are embroidered on the soft blanket and matching red pillowcases. Smaller, heart-shaped red pillows and square pink ones with white lace decorate the head of the bed. The wall beneath the low hanging ceiling is covered with light blue paper.

The raindrops sound as heavy as bricks as they pound against the metal roof. I pull back the curtain to see the rain, but there is no window—just more wall.

Water drips onto the brown linoleum floor next to the vanity. At the front of the room sits an old television and a glass bottle decorated with pictures.

I have a picture frame near my television, too.

The house is in Site C of Khayelitsha, a sprawling shantytown outside of Cape Town established in 1985 as a dumping ground for black families forcibly removed from settlements closer to the city under the Group Areas Act, a key law in the apartheid system that mandated separate living areas based on racial identity.

Today, Khayelitsha is a thriving metropolis in its own right, though it remains a powerful illustration of the poverty that apartheid has left behind. Its name means "our new home" in Xhosa, one of South Africa's eleven official languages, but as many as 50.8 percent of its 329, 002 people were unemployed in 2001, according to a census taken then. Even so, its residents work hard to make it their home.

Pulling up to Vicky's bed and breakfast in a Mercedes tour bus earlier, I was immediately struck by the houses constructed out of scraps of metal and other materials collected from the streets. Pieces of broken glass and garbage covered the gravel ground where children were playing happily, many of them running around without shoes.

As abruptly as the surroundings shook my suburban under-standing of well-being, my attention was captured by the excited screams and waves of children outside Vicky's home.

The children are happy, I saw.

I came to Khayelitsha convinced that the government had failed its citizens. It made promises after its transformation into a democratic state in 1994, but many have yet to be kept.

The government adopted a ground-breaking constitution in 1996, which in Section 26 of its Bill of Rights guarantees: "Everyone has the right to have access to adequate housing. The state must take reasonable legislative and other measures, within its available resources, to achieve the progressive realisation of this right."

I came to Khayelitsha pitying its residents.

My house is made of bricks, I thought. My streets have sidewalks. There is no trash on the ground. The residents of my neighborhood can be fined if they leave animal waste behind.

I wondered where the "real" houses were, thinking about the book titled *Shack Chic* that I had seen in a museum bookstore. I thought the book was a joke, depicting the innovative décor of some of South Africa's shack dwellers.

But as I lay underneath the satin blanket, I began to have second thoughts.

The residents of Khayelitsha were an inspiration to me. Though the government still has a lot of work to do before making a dent in the unemployment rate or mitigating the prevalence of poverty, I admired the people of "Our New Home" for their resilience and perseverance. They had built their homes themselves and they had created the township from the ground up, giving it character and personality and taking pride in their achievements.

Whatever it looked like from the outside, speeding past it on the motorway, from the inside it looked and felt like home.

Riding the Teeter-totter

By Kristin Pitts
Khayelitsha, South Africa

I was ashamed of myself for being so happy to leave.

But the fact is, I was. And not just a little. When our chartered mini-bus pulled into Khayelitsha, I welcomed it, silently.

After two days in one of South Africa's largest black townships, my bangs had become a greasy paste on my forehead. My clothes were covered in a thin layer of dirt. I smelled a lot like body odor and a little like the many layers of deodorant I had used to mask it.

I was happy to see the twenty-one-seat Toyota Coaster, because for this sour, Spring-Breeze-scented girl, the bus symbolized hot water. A shower. Soap. Also, space and alone time and freedom.

Looking back, I realize that I focused so much on what I was going to that I forgot to appreciate what I was leaving behind.

When we had first arrived, Vicky Ntozini welcomed us into the three-bedroom shack that serves as both her home and as South Africa's smallest hotel—Vicky's Bed and Breakfast. Her homemade walls, lined with newspaper articles, pay testament to the world's fascination with her and her desire to bring tourism to an unlikely destination.

We sat in her living room in chairs that varied in color, shape, and comfort as she gave us what I soon learned was the standard speech for visitors. It began with a welcome and ended with her looking at each of us, saying: "You are not here to see how poor we are. You are here to learn."

But I was not quite ready. Although I had been preparing for this trip for months, I was not sure if I was ready for the kind of lessons Vicky was going to teach us. To put it simply, there was a lot to get over.

Outside, barefoot children walked on glass-covered streets. Multicolored shacks, built of tin, cardboard, wood, and any other material available leaned on one another like mismatched dominos and stretched out for miles. Most families' running water, if they had ever had it, was shut off. Never mind heat for the dropping temperatures.

Vicky's education was not the kind I was used to. I felt out of place—uncomfortable—and not just because my needs, like my wants, are so often met, but because poverty was right in front of me, and I was not sure what I was supposed to learn from it.

But before I could show any signs of an official freak-out, Vicky took us out of her house and down the dirt roads of Khayelitsha, stopping every now and then to talk with her neighbors. Within a few feet, we met smiling faces, a few waves, and occasional honks from teenage boys. After about a mile, we met a woman who runs a soup kitchen out of her house for elderly and HIV-positive members of the community. But we had not gone more than a few inches from her doorway when we met the one thing we had been warned about: the kids.

Just as Vicky had predicted, they were everywhere, and they wanted to hold our hands. So there, on the dust-filled roads of Khayelitsha, among women hanging hand-washed laundry and boys playing pick-up soccer, my inner camp counselor came out, a few weeks before I'd anticipated needing it.

A little girl in a stained beige shirt grabbed my hand. I asked what her name was. She told me. It was not Amanda or Kelly or Britney or anything else I recognized. I needed to hear it another time.

I asked again and again, until I got it right and she smiled.

I also wanted to know her age, what subjects she loved to study, and if she knew Miss Marie Mack. But she, and about ten of her friends, had questions for me: What was my name? Did I have a boyfriend? Who did I like better, Shakira or Beyonce?

It felt so good, so right, to be there, interacting with kids and talking with people who were making what looked like a slum into what in many ways is a thriving community. It felt right to take in the township through human interactions, instead of with a click of my camera.

But that night, my warmness, both literally and figuratively, went away. A few other women and I went to stay with a friend of Vicky's, who had offered up her home to us.

We literally put her out of her own bedroom, and though I thanked her, my mind could not stop counting the "flaws." The bed was damp. The corrugated tin roof was leaking in many spots. The floors were uneven, and so were the walls. But what really got me was the bucket in the corner, with two pieces of fabric hanging on its rim.

As soon as the woman left the room, I turned to my roommate Faythe and said something that she still teases me for: "If you pee in that bucket, I'll kill you."

After vowing to one another that the bucket would remain untouched, Faythe and I tried our best to sleep. But nature had other plans. The rain started just a few hours after we got to the house and ended just before we left. That gave it just enough time to find its way through the tin roof and onto the floor, the pillows, and eventually, my forehead.

Cheesy poets and songwriters romanticize the rain. Before that night, I might have become one of them, but after hearing what rain on a tin roof really sounds like, I'll leave those words to be written by someone a little more emo. I had never heard rain like that before, and I hope to never hear it that way again.

I woke up thinking that we were in the midst of a flood, worried that the shack might give way. The next morning, I found out that what I had thought was a thunderstorm was really a light shower, one that left behind only occasional light puddles.

That night I had wrapped my arms so tightly around myself that I was sore for days—a constant reminder of my night in Khayelitsha and the hospitality my self-pity would not let me accept.

That day we got back on our coach bus. Though it was hard to say goodbye, there was a shameful, undeniable part of me that was happy to end my education in Khayelitsha. It is hard to be confronted with your own privilege, and even harder to figure out that you have done nothing to deserve it.

The transition back to "vacation destination South Africa" was awkward. Our tour guide took us to a restaurant, where a buffet lined one wall. Then we went to the Kirstenbosch Botanical Gardens, where unlimited money, time and labor are put into making sure that plants do not just survive, but thrive.

It was fucking ridiculous.

Those plants had more water than most South Africans see in a month. We had just been in a place where we had lifted barefoot children over broken glass, even though their crusted, calloused feet were evidence that they had walked those streets for years. The very reason the kids were able to talk to us so much was because their school was closed; their underpaid teachers were on strike for decent wages. And here we were, looking at these very cared-for, very beautiful, plants.

But I cannot pretend I was constantly appalled by our post-Khayelitsha surroundings. That night we stayed in a waterfront hotel where we each had our own bedroom, our own TV, and a choice of what to eat. The bathrooms were big; there were no more buckets.

I felt guilty for being back in luxury and ashamed for getting comfortable with it so quickly. But the fact is, I loved my new bed. I loved my hot shower. I loved all the things I feel entitled to, but should not.

My friend Beth Maclin called the trip "schizophrenic," and I think that is about right. We were either on one end of the teeter-totter or the other, though I am not sure there were any other options.

Since the trip, I have noticed that people are not sure how to handle the township part when I talk about it. They waver between concern and outrage. It is as though I have been somewhere I should not have been and met people I should have avoided. When they ask what it was like, I am never sure what to say. I get the sense that I am supposed to have a sound bite ready, one that I cannot possibly create.

But it was not "great" or "awesome" or even "okay."

No, we were not allowed out of Vicky's alone, and I was not allowed to walk around with a purse. I learned quickly to keep my jewelry in my bag and to only walk to the convenience store with at least a few children in tow.

But I never felt unsafe. I never felt at risk, and I certainly never felt as though I was in the most dangerous place in the world, as some would have it.

All I know is that there are a lot of reasons to leave Khayelitsha. It is the home to extreme poverty, disparity, and a lack of resources. Its simple existence is the legacy of an oppression that has ended formally, but lives on informally. But though most with the ability to do so leave, people like Vicky stay.

From my home in Boston, where I have the things I need but live in a suburb where neighbors are strangers and doors are locked, I can kind of understand why.

A Walk in a Different Light

By Christina Lenis
Khayletisha, South Africa

The tall buildings and bustling streets of Cape Town began to vanish as my face pressed up against the tour bus window. The beauty of Table Mountain was behind me. The only thing ahead was miles of highway bordered by thousands of shacks on either side. My headphones blared Amy Winehouse as my heavy eyes closed into a deep sleep.

Thirty minutes later, our pudgy Indian tour guide, Badresh Kara, picked up a microphone and announced that we had entered Khayletisha, a township north of Cape Town. My eyes slowly opened, sensitive to the sunlight.

I thought about the comfortable bed I would be sleeping in, and I wondered how many girls I would be sharing my room with. I was hoping for just the one roommate I had had throughout the trip, but considering it was a B&B and smaller than the hotels we had stayed in, I figured there might be more.

The bus shook from side to side as the cement-paved roads gave way to bumpy dirt ones. As we headed farther into the township, the shacks grew closer and closer together—a random assortment of one-story bungalows made from scraps of wood, metal, plastic and other discarded materials. Women in long skirts carried baskets on their heads as children ran alongside our minibus and waved.

My thoughts drifted to what the B&B might look like. I imagined a white-shingled house with a turret overlooking the shacks—similar to B&Bs I had stayed in along the coast of Maine.

Suddenly the bus stopped, and I stood up from my seat and peered out the window as the wind blew a hand-painted sign hanging from the small tin shack that spelled out in brightly colored letters: "Vicky's B&B."

A sharp pain ran up my arm. Is this a joke, I wondered? Am I having a heart attack, or is this seriously where I am staying? I looked frantically at the other girls getting off the bus and soon found myself standing outside, surrounded by a half-dozen intensely curious black children competing for my attention.

Minutes later, I was ushered into the sitting room, which was crammed with mismatched furniture. Its wood walls were covered with newspaper reviews of the inn, postcards from past guests, and a poster-size advertisement for the place.

A plump woman in a fez shook hands with me as I grabbed a seat in a gray fabric-covered reclining chair. When everyone in the group had taken seats, she greeted us warmly. "Welcome!" she said. "When you stepped off that bus and into my home, you were no longer tourists. You are no longer guests, you are part of this community and my home."

Vicky told us she opened her B&B nine years ago to get people to experience township life for themselves. She was tired of the negative stories circulating about Khayletisha and of seeing tourists taking pictures through the windows of their massive buses and then disappearing, as if they had been visiting a zoo.

"We're not animals, we don't eat people," she said. "Why don't they get out of the buses and talk to us?" It was then, she said, that she decided to do township tours, which blossomed into overnight tours and led her to start a B&B. And here we were.

After her greeting, Vicky offered us a tour of the neighborhood. As we made our way back outside, she warned us to not be alarmed by the children who would join us. They would try to hold our hands, she said.

The sharp pain in my arm returned. Children touching me! How awful!

I was a bit irrational about dirt and disease and had never liked children. To me, they were just small, germ-infested creatures. As the walk began, I quickly tried to concoct a way to avoid touching them.

Suddenly, kids began pouring into the streets. Before I had time to stick my hands in my pockets, I felt little fingers grab one of them. They gripped it tight as I peered down into the little girl's big brown eyes. She smiled with such a huge grin that all I could do was smile back, as I released a sigh. Maybe this will not be as bad as I thought.

Vicky led the way, as our group of mostly white Simmons women strolled down the dirt streets taking in our surroundings.

Wall-to-wall shacks bordered the narrow streets, with lines of damp clothes drying in the bright winter sun.

Dozens of children scampered after us, as adults stared and waved and passing vans beeped at us, their mostly male passengers sticking their heads out the windows for a look at our parade. We were as strange a sight to them as they were to us.

In the midst of all this, I kept drifting off into my own reflections until I felt an occasional squeeze at my hand. Looking down, I would see the child whose hand I was holding, as she bent her head as far back as she could to get a good look at my face.

The kids were between the ages of three and ten. They wore brightly colored shirts and jeans. Most were shoeless, though the dirt roads were scattered with trash and broken glass. My classmates and I swung them over the debris to avoid cuts, though they dealt with this on a daily basis and their feet were calloused from years of exposure.

Halfway into our walk, one of the older girls took off her sandals and gave them to a younger child. A rush of emotion came over me as I thought back to the bucket of shoes I carried into the residence hall my freshman year in college—how spoiled I am, I thought. Or am I just lucky?

We stopped outside one small, brightly painted cement house where a heavy-set woman with a fuzzy black beret stepped out and invited us in for a chat. Her home doubled as a soup kitchen for HIV patients, the disabled, and the elderly.

Upon entering, we sat on plastic-covered chairs and couches. But before she told us her story, she coughed several times and apologized for not speaking clearly—she had influenza. My mind raced, thinking: germs, spreading through the air. I kept my hands in my lap and told myself not to touch anything. The last thing I needed was to get sick.

As she spoke, the crisp winter air blew through her home. A relative of hers had recently passed away do to the influenza epidemic and now she was sick, she said, adding that she hoped she would make it through the winter.

I missed most of the rest, as I contemplated my options for health care if I was to get sick during my township stay.

As we headed back to Vicky's, we encountered several older teenage boys playing soccer in the street. One kicked the ball to me. Slightly deflated, it rolled slowly toward me, and I attempted to show off my soccer skills. The boy smiled, did some of his own moves, and kicked it back as the children who had accompanied us played with the rest the group.

One of my friends sat on the steps with four "personal hairdressers" running their fingers through her long auburn hair as they carefully braided it. Another child hung upside down, her feet straddling my friend's neck as she looked up and smiled for a picture.

I ran back into the house, grabbed my video camera, and decided to film the children telling me what they wanted to be when they grew up. The answers varied as they pushed each other out of the way to be on camera first and longest. Each one had a lot to say, and they all loved the attention.

The boys wanted to be police officers. Most of the girls were too shy to be on camera, but one with a Pug-like face, silver earrings and a pink-and-turquoise-striped polo over her jeans swung back and forth on a pole as she balanced one foot on a log and said: "I'm gonna talk right now. When I grow up I'm going to be a hairdresser."

She repeatedly asked to re-do her shot until finally I told the little diva there were others waiting to answer the question. She slogged off for the moment but managed to find me later for more camera time.

After twenty minutes, I put my camera down and walked over to a small tin-roofed garage attached to Vicky's where children were playing hand games and hula-hoops. The kids insisted I join them, so I picked up the pink plastic ring, dropped it around my hips, and began rocking back and forth. It fell to my knees within seconds, though, and my audience giggled as they tried to teach me why I was failing.

After a while I grew tired and dropped onto the curb in front of the B&B, listening to music from a shebeen (bar) across the street as a soft wind blew on my face. But after I closed my eyes for a few seconds and began to drift off with my thoughts from the day, I felt something touch my hair. When I opened my eyes, I found not four but six "personal hairdressers" ready for their next customer—me.

They would not take no for an answer, so I let them work their magic as another little girl made me a chain out of gimp. When she was done, she handed me the orange and green strand and tied it to the zipper on my gray hoodie. I gave her R5 (65¢) as she smiled and ran home to put it away.

An hour later, I found more energy and went outside to play soccer again, running up and down the street as the children ran after me. Soon I had a partner—Zinkona. We played against two other girls—Sirve and Sephanthi. Meanwhile, my friends looked on, knowing my phobias, and looked shocked to see me playing like this with all the children.

They really are not that bad, I thought. And I am just a big kid myself when it comes down to it.

I pointed my finger in the direction I planned on kicking the ball and told Zinkona to go long as I booted it down the street. But Sephanthi got in the way, and the ball hit her hard in the knee. She had no shoes or kneepads on, and the hard ball left a bright mark. Tears rolled down her cheeks as her friends ran over to see if she was okay. I patted her on the back and apologized, but she ran into her house as the other children dispersed.

The last time I had played soccer I was in high school, and I had not stopped to think that I was playing with young children who were not wearing soccer gear. As I walked back to my friends, they shook their heads because I had made a child cry.

I felt awful.

A few minutes later, Sephanthi came running back out of her house wearing sandals. She was ready to play again. I smiled to myself as I realized how strong she was. We played a few more games, and then it was time for dinner.

My classmates and I lined up as Vicky and her children brought out big steaming metal pots. The house was silent as Vicky led us in prayer and then served dinner of perfectly cooked fried chicken, rice and mixed vegetables.

Afterward, we sat around an open space heater and talked until the room assignments were given out. My roommate and I would be sleeping at Vicky's that night. The others would stay in different homes in the neighborhood.

As eight o'clock rolled around, the other girls were escorted to their new quarters, while my roommate and I sat on the couch with Vicky's family watching "The Last Samurai" with her daughter Malande squished between us.

"I like your tackies," she said, pointing at my shoes.

"My what? You think my shoes are tacky?" I said, looking

down at my light blue sneakers.

"No, your tackies. Umm...they're like a shoe," she said.

"Oh, you mean sneakers. Yes, you like my sneakers. Thanks! Here, try one on," I said, taking a shoe off and handing it to her.

She slid her bare foot into it. "These are nice," she said with an impish smile, which showed a few of her upper teeth, as she got off the couch and walked around the room.

"Now I look like you," she laughed, sitting back down and sliding her foot easily out of the shoe. It was a few sizes too big, but in a few years she might grow into it.

We sat in silence as the movie played on. A few minutes later she turned to me and asked, "When are you coming back?"

"I am here until Tuesday," I said.

"No, when are you coming back individually, by yourself?" she said.

I looked at her innocent face, and it hit me: I did not have an answer.

Probably never, and if so, not for many years. This was a once-in-a-lifetime opportunity to experience South Africa and learn about its people. I was not sure when I would get another chance to do it.

As I thought about this, tears began to roll down my cheek. I thought about the people I was with, how happy they were with what to me seemed like the worst of conditions. When Malande asked why I was crying. I tried to play it off because I had no answer.

She wiped my tears and got me some tissues.

As I sat there, the children brought Vicky and her husband dinner. They spoke in Xhosa among themselves, and as they talked I became intensely aware of our cultural differences.

Here I was in a shack in the middle of Africa, as far away from home as I had ever been (and then some), but amidst it all, I was finding the meaning of family. Here were people so different from me who were just sitting around eating and talking and watching a movie on the TV. This could just as easily have been my family.

It was difficult to grasp the concept that people living in what seemed to me such poverty were smiling and wiping my tears away. They were so strong, they had such hope—and sitting there that night, I realized, I was no longer a tourist, no longer a guest, but part of Vicky's family.

Never Forget

By Sheenan Ashley Price
Khayelitsha, South Africa

> In the light of memory and remembering. Through the
> streams of our senses. Reconnecting. Recollecting. We find
> our way home.
> —from *Slave Dream*, by Malika Ndlovu

Eleven adults gather in a small, crowded room for instruction,
silently, patiently waiting for their names to be called.

Attendance is taken. One student is reprimanded for not
following instructions.

"Get your hand up," the teacher shouts. "I don't care if you are
tired. Get that hand up above your head."

The instructor is Malande Ntozini. She is ten.

Her home is nestled in the middle of the bustling Site C
section of Khayelitsha, the largest black township on the outskirts
of Cape Town, a jumbled mix of modest brick and mortar houses
and improvised wood, tin and plastic shacks.

Malande lives with her mother, Vicky Ntozini, a pioneer of
township bed-and-breakfast establishments. Vicky's three-bedroom B&B is the smallest hotel in Cape Town, but it is nearly
always full. Malande is a born leader in a country in the
beginning stages of a profound transition from one of the world's
most extreme forms of racial domination—apartheid—to a
democracy with a constitution that promises not only political but
also social, economic and cultural equality.

And it is children like Malande who say they will ensure its
future. "I am going to first teach the children. Then go study in
New York. Then come back home and teach more children," she
exclaims with certainty.

On this particular day, however, none of the children prepare
for school. A public sector strike has cancelled it for the next
two days. But this does not slow her down or dampen her

enthusiasm—it only shifts her focus of attention to her visitors.

The strike affects many government facilities and services including schools, hospitals, airports, border control, correctional services, police operations and courts, according to the global media service allAfrica.com.

"My teacher told me the strike is about more money—better wages," Malande says.

The Congress of South African Trade Unions (COSATU), South Africa's largest trade union federation with more than two million members, is leading the public sector demand for increased wages. COSATU, a strategic ally of the ruling African National Congress, played a vital role in the fight against apartheid in the 1980s and early 1990s. Today, however, it is challenging its long-standing political partner in the streets over basic bread-and-butter issues, a sign that the legacy of inequality from the apartheid era is far from resolved.

A week into the strike, COSATU leaders say they are prepared to extend the strike for the long haul until the government either accepts its proposal for a 10 percent increase—down from an original demand of 12 percent—or makes a better offer than what has been presented so far, according to published reports. But with the government only upping its counter-offer from 6 to 7.25 percent, the outlook for a quick resolution is slim, which leaves Malande and thousands like her with no school to go to for the foreseeable future. But that is not the only problem she faces in trying to secure an education.

Even when they are open, schools for black South African children lack basic resources, as young children like Malande are acutely aware. "We have forty children in one class. How can one teacher help everyone?" she asks.

But she is also aware that some black children are more equal than others. "The government children have seven in one class," she says.

"It is mostly black schools that are affected—children whose parents cannot afford to take their children to private schools," says Bongi Mkhize, an artist and teacher in Johannesburg. "It means the poor suffer."

Mkhize is a resident of Soweto—a group of black townships southwest of Johannesburg, South Africa's largest city. She teaches in the Johannesburg suburbs.

Mkhize says the education system is different for the black children who attend government schools in the townships than for those who attend private schools, most of whose students are white. "It depends on how much you have or invest for your kids' educations," she says.

The fact that such racial injustice is also a prominent feature of American history is not lost on most South Africans, as is illustrated by a powerful exhibit on the twin struggles for racial equality at Cape Town's historic Slave Lodge, a site frequented by many South African students on field trips.

Although all schools in a given district were often characterized by the authorities as "equal" in mid-twentieth century America, most black schools were far inferior to their white counterparts. Lack of resources, overcrowding, and enormous travel distances were common factors for black students in both the U.S. and South Africa, according to the exhibit, titled "Separate is Not Equal: The Struggle Against Separate Schooling in America" and sponsored by the U.S. Consulate, much to the surprise of many visitors.

The multimedia exhibit starts with the subjugation and domination of blacks by European conquerors in South Africa and moves seamlessly into a pictorial presentation of the experience of African Americans at a time when legal racial segregation in public facilities, including schools, was the norm across America.

Upon entering the museum, a turn to the left takes one on a journey through the history of slavery in the Cape, with an in-depth look at the role it played in the Indian Ocean slave trade. The slaves were brought from four principle areas: India-Ceylon, Indonesia, Mozambique and Madagascar. This influx, coupled with the conquest and decimation of the indigenous San and Khoi peoples by the mainly male European colonists who took wives and concubines from among the conquered peoples, formed the basis for the large "colored" or mixed race population of contemporary Cape Town and its environs, estimated today at four million.

Next, one walks through a long hall with huge, inspiring quotations on its walls, written in a flowing cursive style by influential South Africans. At the end of the walkway is the entrance to the American civil rights exhibit.

A timeline from the 1950s into the late 1960s is displayed on one panel. Martin Luther King's "I have a dream" speech is playing. A room set up to look like a classroom has floor-to-ceiling panels that tell the story of four cases that challenged the segregated school systems across the United States.

A soulful, smoky song plays in the last room, where a visitor is greeted by the disturbing sight of two black men hanging from a tree in a larger than life-size mural painted on the back wall. A white porcelain mannequin stands in a corner draped in the white hooded attire of a Ku Klux Klan member. A small black-and-white television shows a news report from the period. Meanwhile, Billie Holiday belts out "Strange Fruit."

Throughout the museum, the exhibit draws clear parallels between the struggle for democracy waged in South Africa during the apartheid era and that fought by blacks for their rights in America. It also insists to visitors that what they are viewing is not just a slice of history to be filed away and forgotten.

On a cream wall at the end of the exhibit written in dark brown, old English lettering just large enough to make out are the words: "For too long, fear of confronting the shame associated with slavery has played a huge part in the almost collective loss of memory about slavery."

Appendices

SIMMONS COLLEGE

Simmons College is a nationally distinguished, small university in the heart of Boston, Massachusetts, with a 2007/2008 enrollment of close to 5,000. Founded in 1899, Simmons was the first four-year college in the United States to provide both liberal arts and career preparation for women. Today, it has undergraduate programs for women and graduate programs for women and men, including the world's only graduate business program designed specifically for women; co-ed graduate schools of library and information science, health studies, and social work; and co-ed graduate programs in education, communications management and liberal arts.

Academics

The undergraduate College of Arts and Sciences, from which all but one of the participants in the South Africa project were drawn, has 2,000 students, more than a fifth of whom are self-identified members of ethnic minorities. The school is best known for its distinctive emphasis on pre-professional education that prepares students for the working world. It combines a traditional liberal arts education with courses tailored to future vocations. Students are also required to take interdisciplinary courses in writing, art, literature, language, history, scientific inquiry, quantitative reasoning and ethics, among others.

Simmons offers degrees in a wide range of disciplines, with more than forty majors and programs. Among the most popular are psychology, communications, political science/international relations, nursing, management, biology/pre-med and English. Interdisciplinary majors include Africana and women's studies; among the many minors is one in social justice. Distinguished faculty include noted researchers, authors, and experts who are passionately dedicated to teaching. While the curriculum is challenging, small classes and a collaborative environment facilitate student success.

Students expand classroom work and prepare for the world after college through independent study, usually an off-campus internship. The requirement—a hallmark of a Simmons education—challenges them to approach a problem, project or workplace experience as independent researchers and applied learners. This gives them a rigorous intellectual experience that enables them to attain both depth and practice in their chosen disciplines, to sustain a longer-term project of their own initiative, and to connect their academic work with future employment or graduate study.

Students acquire a global outlook by studying languages, cultures, and foreign policies and by taking advantage of foreign study opportunities, including short-term travel courses, such as the one to South Africa, and half- or full-year study abroad programs. Simmons is a member of the Colleges of the Fenway consortium, which includes Wentworth Institute of Technology, Wheelock College, Emmanuel College, Massachusetts College of Pharmacy and Health Sciences, and the Massachusetts College of Art. The New England Philharmonic is the College's orchestra-in-residence.

Campus Life

Boston, the largest and oldest of the New England region's many cities, is rich in history, tradition and cultural diversity. It attracts more than 250,000 undergraduate and graduate students from around the world every year, making it the nation's largest "college town." As an urban institution deeply involved in and committed to the city, Simmons places many students in field-based work at neighborhood institutions as part of their regular courses of study. Fully 30 percent participate in off-campus service learning.

Simmons is located between Boston's lively Fenway district and the Longwood Medical Area, a world-renowned hub for research and health care. More than half the student body lives in nine campus residence halls and three off-site locations. They take advantage of a vibrant urban community of colleges, research centers, museums, sports stadiums, restaurants, shops, and performance venues in a neighborhood that is the soul of the city.

College women compete in eight NCAA Division III varsity intercollegiate sports: basketball, crew, field hockey, soccer, swimming, diving, tennis, and volleyball. Simmons also belongs to the Great Northeast Athletic Conference (GNAC) and the Eastern Collegiate Athletic Conference (ECAC) and is affiliated with the Massachusetts Association of Intercollegiate Athletics for Women (MAIAW).

A wide variety of academic and other campus organizations involve students of all types. Academic clubs appeal to students interested in communications, psychology, biology/pre-med, math/computer science, and other fields. Other organizations include language and culture, performing arts, student government, honor societies, publications, entertainment, international and multicultural student associations, religious groups, and community service opportunities, as well as activist groups like Amnesty International, Students Taking Action Now: Darfur (STAND), and the Student Labor Action Project (SLAP).

South Africa Project's Academic Sponsors

The ten-person student group that produced the articles for this book did so for an advanced writing course jointly sponsored by the Department of Communications and the Department of Political Science/International Relations. The four-person team that produced the book did so for an advanced studio course also under the Department of Communications.

Department of Communications

The mission of the Department of Communications is to provide an intellectually broadening path of study of the media and preparation for the communications profession. Faculty are committed to standards of excellence and to the creation of a climate where students strive to make a difference in the community. The program emphasizes the development of critical thinking and problem solving, superior writing capabilities, a contemporary visual intelligence, effective oral communication, and technical competence in the digital age.

Students actively engage with the challenge of communication for the screen, the airwaves, the page, and the Web while gaining an understanding of the impact of the media on society and the individual and the influence of media convergence on the practice of communications. These objectives are accomplished through a supportive environment of collaboration, creativity, and active engagement with experiential learning, led by a faculty of professionals and scholars.

The communications major provides a foundation in the study of written, visual, aural and electronic media. Areas of specialization allow students to take developmental coursework in one area within the field. This program culminates in advanced coursework and capstone experiences like internships, independent study, and Studio Five—the department's student-run, professional communications workplace that designed and laid out this book. Journalism students are also encouraged to participate in the weekly campus newspaper, *The Simmons Voice*, and a new Web-based radio station.

The major prepares students for employment in a great variety of positions dealing with communications-related problems and opportunities that face contemporary businesses and organizations. Typical career paths include publishing, print and broadcast journalism, public relations, advertising, video, graphic, Web, and multimedia design and production.

Department of Political Science/International Relations

Part of a liberal arts education is exposure to a plurality of perspectives and values and an encouragement of civil and rational discourse amidst fundamental disagreement. The Department of Political Science and International Relations offers two majors designed toward these ends.

The political science curriculum includes a senior integrative seminar where students reflect on how the major subfields and ideological approaches of the discipline relate to a common topic. The capstone integrative seminar for international relations majors, taught by a distinguished practitioner in international affairs who holds the "Warburg Chair in International Relations," encourages students to combine conceptual and content-based knowledge with policy applications. This major encourages responsible world citizenship that recognizes both the historically and politically contingent nature of geographic and political divisions and the perennial dilemmas of theorizing beyond borders.

Both majors gain real-life experience through internships in legislative and governmental offices, domestic and international nongovernmental organizations (NGOs), and the international sectors of corporations and financial institutions. In 2004, twelve students studied the American presidential selection process and spent an intense two weeks at the Democratic National Convention in Boston in hands-on activities and internships. In 2007, fourteen students spent six weeks in Washington, D.C., studying the workings of the federal government, public policy-making, interest groups, and social movements.

The department also administers the new Barbara Lee Fellows Program, which attracts strong students from several majors who compete for fellowships leading to mentoring relationships with area legislators, and it supports study and interning abroad, with faculty members taking students on foreign study experiences to France, Egypt, Thailand, China, and Japan and working to foster links across the College like those that paired Communications and Political Science/International Relations students in the South Africa project.

The Itinerary:
May 21–June 10
Johannesburg

Monday, May 21

Arrival in South Africa and check-in at the
Melville Turret Guest House.

Tuesday, May 22

Morning meeting with Soweto Electricity Crisis Committee
Director Trevor Ngwane and day-long tour of Soweto, with
visits to the Regina Mundi Church and the Hector Pieterson
Museum, lunch at Wandi's, and a stop at the Nelson Mandela
Museum, as well as a walk through an informal squatter
settlement and a drive through the township's middle and upper
class neighborhoods.

Wednesday, May 23

Morning excursion to Ormonde for a half-day visit
to the Apartheid Museum.

Lunch at the University of Witwatersrand and a briefing
with journalism department chair Anton Harber.

Afternoon meeting with gender activist, author and
former *Speak* editor Shamim Meer.

Evening meeting with refugees and exiles from Eritrea
on their experiences in South Africa and their homeland,
organized by the Johannesburg chapter of the Eritrean
Movement for Democracy and Human Rights.

Thursday, May 24

Morning tour of Constitution Hill and the Constitutional Court before meeting Justice Albie Sachs and touring the judges' chambers and the court's extensive art collection with Sachs' legal researcher, Frank Pelser.

Dinner at Gramadoelus Restaurant with traditional Afrikaner dishes.

Evening at the Market Theatre to see South African Director Yael Farber's "MoLoRa," a re-interpretation of apartheid and its legacy through the Greek classic "Oresteia."

Friday, May 25

A morning meeting with South African Human Rights Commission chair Jody Kollapen.

A half-day visit to the Funda Community College in Soweto with Wits fine arts professor David Andrews, hosted by Funda arts program director Charles Nkosi, Presenters included artists Bangile Mkhize, Thulisile Shongwe, Thandi Dayel, Mathibe Mthite, Flora More, Zanole Nyaka, and Pauline Mazibuko.

Saturday, May 26

Drive to Pilanesberg National Park, check in at Manyane Rest Camp, and a dusk safari through the game reserve.

Sunday, May 27

A dawn safari in an open vehicle, and then a day at the park.

Monday, May 28

Return to Johannesburg and departure on overnight Shosholoza Meyl train to Cape Town.

Cape Town

Tuesday, May 29

Arrival in mid-afternoon, check-in at Protea Hotel Cape Castle.

Wednesday, May 30

A half-day tour of the Malay community in the Bo-Kapp neighborhood led by Tana Baru Tours director and former underground ANC activist Shereen Habib, followed by tea and traditional refreshments at Habib's house.

Afternoon visit to the University of Cape Town hosted by South African College of Music's Paul Sedres, including a campus walk-through and a meeting with the local chapter of Amnesty International.

Evening meeting with refugees and exiles from Eritrea on their experiences in South Africa and their homeland, organized by the Cape Town chapter of Eritreans for Democracy and Human Rights.

Thursday, May 31

A morning visit to the District Six Museum and a meeting in Langa with the chair of the Western Cape Anti-Eviction Committee, Gerty Square, followed by a tour of the Cape Flats.

Afternoon briefing and discussion at the U.S. Consulate on American programs and policy in South Africa led by Consul General Helen La Lime.

Friday, June 1

Cable car excursion to the summit of Table Mountain.

Tour of the Company Gardens and the old Slave Lodge.

Saturday, June 2

Free day.

Sunday, June 3

Transfer to Vicky's Place, a family-run B&B in Khayelitsha township's Site C, for a two-night home-stay.

Monday, June 4

Morning meeting with the Treatment Action Campaign in Khayelitsha's Site B and a tour of the Simelela Centre for rape survivors.

Lunch at Lelapa Restaurant in Langa and a walking tour of the township, including rehabbed apartheid-era single-sex dormitories.

Tuesday, June 5

Full-day excursion to Kirstenbosch Botanical Gardens and the Cape Point Nature Reserve with lunch at the Blue Marlin Restaurant and a stop at the Boulders Beach penguin colony.

Transfer to the Breakwater Lodge near Cape Town's Victoria & Albert Waterfront.

Wednesday, June 6

Half-day excursion to Robben Island where Nelson Mandela and other prominent anti-apartheid activists were jailed for decades.

Thursday-Saturday, June 7–9

Independent research and small group interviews.

Sunday, June 10

Morning visit to the Green Point flea market.

Late afternoon departure for Boston.

Contacts in South Africa

Johannesburg

Soweto Electricity Crisis Centre
Trevor Ngwane
P.O. Box 476
Orlando East, Soweto 1804, S.A.

University of the Witwatersrand
Journalism Department
Anton Harber
Private Bag 4
WITS (Johannesburg) 2050, S.A.
anton@harber.co.za

Shamim Meer
56 Fifth Avenue
Mayfair (Johannesburg) 2108, S.A.
shamim@iafrica.com

EMDHR
Haileab Kidane
P.O. Box 30583
Sunnyside (Pretoria) 0132, S.A.
yayino@yahoo.com

Constitutional Court
Justice Albie Sachs
Frank Pelser, Legal Researcher
Constitution Hill
Private Bag X1
Braamfontein (Johannesburg) 2017, S.A.

Sachs@concourt.org.za
Pelser@concourt.org.za

S.A. Human Rights Commission
Jody Kollapen, Chairperson
Private Bag 2700
Houghton (Johannesburg) 2041, S.A.
c/o MMoletsane@sahrc.org.za

FUNDA
Charles Nkosi, Founder/Director
Artists: Bangile Mkhize, Thulisile Shongwe,
Thandi Dayel, Mathibe Mthite, Flora More,
Zanole Nyaka, Pauline Mazibuko
P.O. Box 2056
Southdale (Soweto) 2135, S.A.

David Andrews
Wits School of Arts
University of the Witwatersrand
Private Bag x3
WITS (Johannesburg) 2050, S.A.
David.Andrew@wits.ac.za

Cape Town

Jedek Travel
Thana Nel
(also guides Kim Dennett, Abe Mongane, Badresh Kara)
32 Firgrove Way
Constantia (Cape Town) 7806, S.A.
Thana@jedek.com

Tana Baru Tours
Shereen Habib
3 Morris Street
Schottschekloof
Cape Town 8018, S.A.
info@bokaap.co.za

University of Cape Town
S.A. College of Music
Private Bag X3
Rondebosch (Cape Town) 7701, S.A.
Paul Sedres
Paul.Sedres@uct.ac.za

EMDHR
c/o Buruk Tekle
P.O. Box 3004
Cape Town 8000, S.A.

Western Cape Anti-Eviction Campaign
Gertrude Square
20 Waratan Street
High Places Eerste River
Cape Town 7100, S.A.
aec@antieviction.org.za

U.S. Consulate
Consul General Helen La Lime
Post Net Suite 50
Private Bag x26
Tokai (Cape Town) 7966, S.A.
c/o Paul Patin, Public Affairs Officer
patinpb@state.gov

Vicky's Place
Vicky Ntozini
C-685A Kiyane St.
Khayelitsha (Cape Town) 7784, S.A.
vickysbandb@yahoo.com

Treatment Action Campaign (TAC)
Town One Properties
Sulani Drive, Site B
Khayelitsha (Cape Town) 7784, S.A.
info@tac.org.za

Notes on the Contributors

Paula Bettencourt (Pawtucket, Rhode Island)
Bettencourt graduated from Simmons in May 2007 with majors in Economics and International Relations.

Lucía Cordón (Guatemala City)
Cordón, a junior, is a member of the Honors Program majoring in both Communications and Political Science, with a minor in History. She has been the Assistant News Editor for *The Simmons Voice* and, in Guatemala, a staff writer for *el Periodico* and an executive board member for the Habitat for Humanity youth group.

Erika Fields (Woburn, Massachusetts)
Fields is a senior majoring in Communications with concentrations in integrated media, writing, and public relations. She sits on the Student Government Association and the executive board of the Campus Activities Board and has served as photo-editor for *The Simmons Voice*.

Elena Larson (Worcester, Massachusetts)
Larson graduated from Simmons in 2007 with a degree in English and Women's Studies. She wrote her honors thesis on location and identity in the novels of South African author Nadine Gordimer. She is currently working on a master's degree in Literary and Cultural Studies at Carnegie Mellon University, Pittsburgh, Penn.

Victoria Latto (Acton, Massachusetts)
Latto is a senior majoring in Sociology with minors in English and Women's Studies. She has published her poetry in *Sidelines* and is active in the annual production of "The Vagina Monologues." She has also volunteered at the day shelter Women's Lunch Place.

Christina Lenis (Worcester, Massachusetts)

Lenis is a junior majoring in Communications with a concentration in public relations and marketing and a minor in English. She has served as the Business Manager and a columnist for *The Simmons Voice* and sits on the executive boards of the Public Relations Student Society of America and Students Take Action Now Darfur.

Beth Maclin (Waterford, Connecticut)

Maclin is a senior majoring in Political Science and Communications, with a focus on writing. She has served as president of Amnesty International and Editor-in-Chief of *The Simmons Voice* and is the student representative to the Committee for a Simmons Initiative on Human Rights/Social Justice. She aspires to be a foreign correspondent in Africa.

Faythe Mallinger (Pittsburgh, Pennsylvania)

Mallinger is a senior from and a member of the Honors Program majoring in Philosophy with a minor in English. She is a member of the HIV/AIDS Awareness Program and volunteers at a nonprofit organization in the Boston area. After graduation she plans to pursue a career in the legal profession.

Kristin Pitts, (Olathe, Kansas)

Pitts is a senior majoring in Communications with a concentration in writing. She has written and edited for six publications, including *The Simmons Voice*, *Teen Voices*, and *The Kansas City Star*. She has served as a First-Year Experience facilitator, writing tutor, Student Government Association senator, and Amnesty International vice president.

Sheenan Ashley Price (Grand Prairie, Texas)

Price, a 2004 graduate of Spelman College with a major in Sociology, is pursuing dual master's degrees in Education and Gender and Cultural Studies on oral histories of black women's survival strategies. She coordinated the Boston Cares program for the Scott Ross Center for Community Service and spent 2007-2008 teaching in Madrid, Spain.

Acknowledgments

We are deeply grateful for the time South Africans put into making this project such an enriching experience when they have so much else to deal with, not only in their efforts to make real the vision of a democratic, rights-based society but also to cope with the daunting demands of daily life. Some who assisted us appear in these articles; others do not. Some are listed in the appendix; many are not. To all who helped, listed or not: a heartfelt thanks.

A handful deserve special mention for arranging meetings, outings and exposures: Shamim Meer, Frank Pelser (Constitutional Court), David Andrew (Wits/Funda), Paul Sedres (UCT), Paul Patin (U.S. Consulate), and Thana Nell (Jedek Travel).

Thanks to Simmons dean Diane Raymond for scaring up the resources to make it happen and to Communications Department chair Jim Corcoran and Political Science/International Relations Department chair Cheryl Welch for helping plan the project and supporting it throughout. Also to Robin Melavalin in the study abroad office and Joe Roma at Intrax for help with logistics and to publisher Kassahun Checole for making this book a reality.

Special thanks to Studio 5, a Simmons communications seminar, for the outstanding work they did in designing and laying out the book. Melanie Klaus-Martin, Nikki Panagiotaris, Kady Shea, and Sheila Sheedy went way above and beyond their classroom obligations to make this a success.

We are also grateful to Jessica Rudis and Jennifer Rheaume for their meticulous copyediting and to the Studio 5 professors who mentored the project: Sarah Burrows and Ellen Grabiner.

About the Editor:
Dan Connell

Dan Connell (www.danconnell.net) is a Distinguished Lecturer in Journalism and African Politics at Simmons College, Boston, and the author or editor of nine books, including *Against All Odds: Chronicles of the Eritrean Revolution* (1997), *Rethinking Revolution: New Strategies for Democracy & Social Justice: The Experiences of Eritrea, South Africa, Palestine & Nicaragua* (2002), *Conversations with Eritrean Political Prisoners* (2005), and *Women to Women; Young Americans in South Africa* (2006).